AADHAAR

AADHAAR

A Biometric History of
INDIA'S 12-DIGIT
REVOLUTION

SHANKKAR AIYAR

HarperCollins *Publishers* India

First published by Westland Publication Ltd 2017

This edition published in India by HarperCollins *Publishers* 2024
4th Floor, Tower A, Building No. 10, DLF Cyber City,
DLF Phase II, Gurugram, Haryana – 122002
www.harpercollins.co.in

2 4 6 8 10 9 7 5 3 1

Copyright © Shankkar Aiyar 2017, 2024

P-ISBN: 978-93-5699-314-3
E-ISBN: 978-93-5699-317-4

The views and opinions expressed in this book are the author's own and the facts are as reported by him, and the publishers are not in any way liable for the same.

Shankkar Aiyar asserts the moral right to
be identified as the author of this work.

All rights reserved. No part of this publication may be reproduced, stored in a retrieval system, or transmitted, in any form or by any means, electronic, mechanical, photocopying, recording or otherwise, without the prior permission of the publishers.

Typeset in 11/15 Sabon by
SÜRYA, New Delhi

Printed and bound at
Nutech Print Services - India

This book is printed on FSC® certified paper
which ensures responsible forest management.

For
my parents
Mangalam and Venkatramani
for the foundation

The detailed notes pertaining to this book are available on the HarperCollins *Publishers* India website. Scan this QR code to access the same.

Contents

Introduction — ix
AN UPDATE ON INDIA'S 12-DIGIT REVOLUTION

Preface — xxv
WHY AND WHY NOW

1. Who I Am — 1
   THE BIRTH OF AADHAAR AND THE NEED FOR IT

2. Start Up in Sarkar — 23
   HOW TO GET GOING IN GOVERNMENT

3. The Know Who Factor — 52
   KNOW HOW NEEDS POLITICAL AIR COVER

4. Push for the Pull — 81
   IDENTIFYING IDEAS FOR ACCELERATION

5. Law and Political Order — 101
   WHO IS UIDAI, ASKS THE OPPOSITION

6. The Politics of Politics — 118
   ASCENT OF DISSENT, DISPUTES AND DIFFERENCES

7. Modification — 149
   PM MAKES IDENTITY THE PRIME PLATFORM

Epilogue — 193
RIGHT TO PRIVACY AND GETTING IT RIGHT

Notes — 229
Acknowledgements — 230

Introduction

AN UPDATE ON INDIA'S 12-DIGIT REVOLUTION

When I first defined the concept of Aadhaar as India's 12-digit revolution, eyebrows arched in scepticism. Aadhaar was then viewed as yet another programme to enable identity, and 'revolution' appeared to them far-fetched from reality. In less than seven years since this book was first published, released by President Pranab Mukherjee and received by Prime Minister Narendra Modi, Aadhaar has come to be the foundation of the world's largest human-scale digital public infrastructure. It's a concept that is applauded and recommended globally.

Traditionally, a sit-rep – situation report or update – would be an addendum. It is being placed upfront for context – and perspective. Aadhaar began its journey as an idea backed by technology, which promised to address complex economic challenges. It was designed to fill a peculiarly Indian vacuum. Millions of Indians lacked documentation to prove their identity. The challenge of proving 'I am who I say I am' derailed delivery of welfare,

Introduction

detained access to services and imposed hardships. The government spent billions but did not know and could not certify that the welfare was reaching the intended beneficiary. Aadhaar was conceptualised to enable last mile of delivery and accountability.

This is indeed a revolution. The transformation is best illustrated by the scale of adoption and utility. Much has changed since the issue of the first Aadhaar to a resident of the tiny village of Tembhli in Maharashtra. Over 1,381 million persons have been enrolled on the world's largest biometric identity platform. Think about the scale – that is 1,381 million names, 1,381 million addresses, 1,381 million photographs, 2,762 million irises and over 13 billion fingerprints. Think about the simplicity of design. Everyone has a number backed by biometrics. The biometric system banishes ghosts – the bane of identity systems in advanced economies.

In the past decade, the digitally verifiable ID system has helped people state who they are, and access benefits and services across all three tiers of government. Aadhaar has also enabled engagement between consumers and providers. Every day, over 80 million Aadhaar holders deploy the 12-digit number to authenticate their identity. As of 10 October 2023, the Aadhaar platform has enabled 101,100 million authentications. The platform has empowered citizens, enabled governments and powered efficiency.

Look at the scale of usage. India runs the world's largest food security programme under the National Food Security Act, 2013. It provides ration to over 810 million

Introduction

people across rural and urban India. Over 99.7 per cent of the ration cards are linked with Aadhaar. The rural employment programme Mahatma Gandhi National Rural Employment Guarantee Scheme (MGNREGS) is located at the intersection of urban and rural economy. It is designed to provide 100 days of employment at a specified minimum wage. Over 91 per cent of the 265 million persons registered are enrolled on Aadhaar. The adoption of Aadhaar prevents diversion, eradicates fakes, enables authentication of identity and ensures delivery of wages.

Aadhaar has effectively engineered a trifecta – the pathway for ease of governance, ease of business and ease of living. Take the challenge of financial inclusion. In 2014, seven decades after India's independence, millions of households lacked access to a bank account to save and to finance their business ambitions. The system required them to prove their identity, which they could not. On 15 August 2014, Prime Minister Narendra Modi announced the launch of Pradhan Mantri Jan Dhan Yojana. The key element designing the success of the programme was deployment of Aadhaar. In nine years, over 500 million persons have been brought into the formal banking system.

This sea change enabled by Aadhaar is underlined in a 2019 study, *The Design of Digital Financial Infrastructure: Lessons from India*, published by the Bank of International Settlements. It points out: 'Given the low levels of both financial inclusion and formal identification in 2008, the magnitude of the challenges facing India

Introduction

a little more than a decade ago was clearly immense. Based on the bank account data and the relationship with GDP per capita discussed above, one rough estimate is that it would have taken 47 years to achieve 80% of adults with a bank account had India solely relied on traditional growth processes.' The expansion of access to banking delivered gender and social inclusion. Nearly 56 per cent of Jan Dhan account holders are women and around 67 per cent of the Jan Dhan accounts are in rural and semi-urban areas. Jan Dhan accounts, essentially belonging to the poorest of the poor, now host a sum of Rs 2.03 lakh crore. Jan Dhan account holders have insurance cover of Rs 1 lakh and are issued a Rupay debit card. The expansion of financial inclusion enabled direct benefit transfer of LPG subsidies, pensions, scholarships and targeted welfare to the bank of accounts of beneficiaries.

Aadhaar has also facilitated ease of business and ease of living. A major hurdle for banks opening no frills and regular accounts was the cost of acquisition. Aadhaar has facilitated speed and lower costs. The consumer can open an account in a day as compared to weeks earlier. Speed has shrunk costs to a fraction. Finance Minister Nirmala Sitharaman, speaking on India's digital public infrastructure in Washington, pointed out that Aadhaar brought down the cost of know your customer (KYC) from as high as Rs 700 to Rs 3, or in international terms from $ 9 to a few cents. This has also brought down cost of loan processing by almost 75 per cent. Aadhaar has made life easier for those accessing telecom services.

Introduction

In the earlier regime it would take a person a week or more – the process stretched from filling forms for proof of identity and proof of address to physical authentication of identity and validation of addresses. Aadhaar-enabled eKYC has reduced friction for both usage and delivery of services.

Success didn't come without attendant controversy. The introduction of Aadhaar as a mechanism to enable the contract between the people and the state triggered binary debates and public interest litigation. The opposition charged the Manmohan Singh government with proceeding without legislative backing. Such was the magnitude of political resistance that the BJP while in opposition had sworn to cancel Aadhaar when they came to power. The adoption and expansion of Aadhaar following the advent of the Modi government (detailed in the chapter 'Modification') represents the triumph of pragmatism over political rhetoric. The Aadhaar Act of 2016 provides statutory status for the use of Aadhaar as an instrument 'to provide for, as a good governance, efficient, transparent, and targeted delivery of subsidies, benefits and services, the expenditure for which is incurred from the Consolidated Fund of India'. There were legitimate fears of an overreach by the State, the spectre of an Orwellian state. This book traces the social, political and legal issues and how they came to be resolved. The demands for safeguarding privacy were examined and validated by the judiciary. Privacy is scaffolded by the landmark judgement of the Supreme Court of India issued in September 2018. The Court's ruling on *Puttaswamy vs Union of India* states, 'The

Introduction

requirement under Aadhaar Act to give one's demographic and biometric information does not violate fundamental right of privacy.' The nine-judge bench also underlined, 'The State while enlivening right to food, right to shelter etc. envisaged under Article 21 cannot encroach upon the right of privacy of beneficiaries nor former can be given precedence over the latter.' The judgment is essentially the red line on privacy neither private nor public institutions dare cross. Critically, the judgment made de jure what was de facto and created mass awareness on the fundamental right of privacy.

It is now established that Aadhaar has catalysed transformation across sectors. The milestones of transformation were enabled by design and propelled by serendipity. Pramod Varma, the former chief architect of Aadhaar, describes the approach eloquently. In a conversation with the author, he defines the crux as 'minimalistic building blocks for enabling the ecosystem to engineer solutions'. Aadhaar is an essential ingredient in the recipe of solutions.

Aadhaar has catalysed India's digital physical infrastructure (DPI) to enable governance. The DPI platform has aided efforts to address both supply- and demand-side issues. Characteristically in the government, size matters and solutions are often about capital expenditure. In stark contrast, the Aadhaar team focussed on engineering minimal building blocks – not maximal solutions – which could be leveraged by the ecosystem to drive incentives. The key was to align innovation and policy – a good illustration is the acceleration of

Introduction

enrolment following linking of Aadhaar with LPG subsidies. Sustainability was critical as innovations would collapse without mass subscription or adoption.

The strategy has been to address friction in the system – between citizens and government and between consumers and providers. At every step the key was to leverage existing regulatory landscape and build innovation on it. For instance, the Reserve Bank of India (RBI) had already allowed one-time-password authentication for mobile wallets. This enabled the policy to use Aadhaar authentication to enable banks to open no-frills Jan Dhan accounts. India had enacted a law to allow digital signatures under the IT Act of 2003 and a regulatory system under the Controller of Certifying Authority. This opened up the scope for creating the facility for eSign, allowing millions of Aadhaar holders to use digital signature within a paperless workflow. India has a colonial era addiction of document-based engagement with government and enterprises. This created friction and imposed costs on both users and providers. The Aadhaar platform afforded the creation of DigiLocker. The DigiLocker is effectively a personal folder in cloud enabling citizens to store digital documents and credentials – Aadhaar cards, vaccine certificates, mark sheets, driving licence, et al. – which, when necessary, can also be shared and verified digitally, eliminating costly paper-based verification.

In 2016, the *Economic Survey* presented the potential of JAM – an acronym symbolising the blend of Jan Dhan, Aadhaar and Mobile telephony in delivery of services and welfare. The proof of concept was tested soon enough.

Introduction

In November 2016, the Modi government demonetised Rs 500 and Rs 1,000 notes. The move sucked out over Rs 15.4 trillion of a total of Rs 16.9 trillion of currency in circulation: roughly 87 per cent of all the cash in the system. The economy came to a virtual standstill and life and livelihoods were threatened.

Flashback 2013 Koramangala, Bengaluru. Nandan Nilekani, chairman of Unique Identification Authority of India (UIDAI), Dilip Asbe who is MD and CEO of National Payments Corporation of India and Pramod Varma are having one of their brainstorming sessions. They ask what more could be done to reduce friction between entities – governments, customers and businesses. Team Nilekani, Asbe and Varma identify payments as a major gap. India's payments universe had two parallel systems. Banks were enabling direct payments via bank accounts between individuals and between individuals and institutions through National Electronic Fund Transfer (NEFT)/Immediate Payment Service (IMPS). There was also the Aadhaar Enabled Payment System (AEPS) for transactions between government and beneficiaries as also between banks and beneficiaries. The missing part was an easy-to-use interface to enable instant payment between entities and people.

To address this gap, the team designed the Unified Payments Interface. The first draft presentation deck was put forth by Varma in September 2014. The team made a presentation at a workshop held at the MCA in Mumbai organised by the National Payments Corporation of India (NCPI). The concept illustrated the capabilities –

Introduction

immediate 24×7 transfers through mobile devices, single click two-factor authentication, and QR code to cover transactions. The concept was well received – it made sense as it came at the intersection of smartphone usage and the advent of cheap 3G connectivity. This prompted trials and the RBI acted in concert with NPC to enable systemic and regulatory changes.

Unified Payments Interface (UPI) was test launched in April 2016 and by August 2016, UPI-enabled Apps were on Google Play Store. India's digital payments system is the envy of the world. The scale of adoption and acceleration in transactions is manifest in data. The RBI's Annual Report reveals generation of UPI quick response (QR) codes increased by 48.4 per cent by end of March 2023 – and it is estimated the number of QR Codes could be as high as 256 million. In September 2023, UPI processed over 10.5 billion transactions. Indeed, on an average, UPI facilitates over 8 billion transactions every month. The facility of UPI is now available to NRIs and even foreign nationals while in India. The RBI is also working on interlinking UPI with Fast Payment Systems of other countries to enable both foreign inward and outward remittances.

The UPI platform also functions as the backbone of FASTag – a contactless system for vehicles to pay toll on highways. The system, which was engineered at NPCI under the leadership of Asbe with the design help of Nilekani and Varma, now facilitates movement of vehicles on India's highways. FASTag can be accessed across 38 banks, records over 10 million transactions

Introduction

a day and seamlessly collects over Rs 5,000 crore in a month. In the days ahead, FASTag could well emerge as the platform for futuristic uses – from parking charges to highway fines, from battery swaps to e-charging costs.

The Aadhaar-based architecture came to India's rescue when the COVID-19 pandemic hit the world. Advanced economies across the world struggled to find mechanisms to transfer welfare and stimulus to citizens. India, blessed with the payment infrastructure, was ready. The Government of India leveraged the Aadhaar-based direct benefit transfer (DBT) platform to remit over Rs 27,442 crore in just three weeks to 114.2 million beneficiaries – indeed it created a record of sorts with 21 million transactions in a single day on 30 March 2020.

The Aadhaar-based DBT system is now the backbone of India's welfare delivery system. The umbrella covers 313 schemes administered by 53 government departments in the Union government. Till date, a sum of over Rs 32.55 lakh crore has been disbursed – in 2023–24 alone, over Rs 2.70 lakh crore has been disbursed. It is not just the Union government. The NPCI's portal shows that state governments too have leveraged the efficiency of DBT. The NPCI portal reveals there are over 7,000 user codes registered against schemes administered by the state government where payments are routed through DBT. Most critically, the use of DBT has inducted efficient last mile delivery and created savings for government. In July 2023, the government informed Parliament that use of DBT has translated into savings of over Rs 2 lakh crore in the past five years.

Introduction

Aadhaar also came to be the go-to platform for managing population-scale interventions. Consider the success of vaccination. Months before the arrival of the vaccine, in October 2020, Nilekani pointed out that if India's economy is to open up, the population would need to be vaccinated. Vaccinating an entire population would be a huge mission. Given the population of 1.3 billion, assuming two doses meant 2.6 billion doses translated to over a 100 million vaccinations a month. The scale of the challenge demanded the design of a digital infrastructure for registration and vaccination. Nilekani funded an open source initiative and asked Varma if he could design the basic concept for the architecture for a capability which would encompass all the steps from registration to vaccination to issue of certificates.

The idea was accepted by the government as the foundation for the birth of COWIN – aka COVID-19 Vaccine Intelligence Network – which was led by R.S. Sharma who was the director general of UIDAI and the current CEO of the National Health Authority. The COWIN platform was set up in a record time of three months – for sure, the concept went through several iterations and endured the challenges of implementation in India's systemic landscape. The platform was inaugurated in January 2021 by the prime minister. Vaccination was opened up first for frontline workers and in phases for the rest of the population. India set a record as the COWIN platform enabled the delivery and certification of over 2 billion doses. Yet again, the foundational base of Aadhaar proved to be critical.

Introduction

The revolution is marching on. New ambitious ideas being rolled out include the Online Network for Digital Commerce, or ONDC, and account aggregator (AA) networks. The ONDC, as it is better known, is an aspirational idea built at the intersection of economics and technology leveraging the open source Beckn Protocol. The world knows of systems that are based on apps – which are platforms. Then there are networks. For instance, X, formerly known as Twitter, is a platform – the internet is a network. There are many payment platforms/apps and then there is UPI, which is a network that connects all players. The ONDC is the engineering of a network which offers sellers and buyers of goods and services, whether the person is in Araria or Ahmedabad, the opportunity to engage in commerce. Nilekani believes ONDC will propel India's e-commerce and estimates that it will grow exponentially from 80 million monthly transacting users to over 500 million in a short time.

The second ambitious idea germinates from the potential of data as an asset. Every individual creates a record of transactions which can be leveraged to show the person/entity's credit potential. The AA network is a data-sharing system that could revolutionise financial engagement by giving consumers access and control over their financial records. A common hurdle faced by individuals and micro, small and medium enterprises is the lack of collateral to negotiate a credit facility. This imposes unusually high interest costs on borrowers. The AA network promotes data as collateral. The control and leverage of data as an asset empowers them to access

Introduction

credit and better financial terms. Indeed earlier this year, the World Bank in its series *Let's Talk Development* observed, 'India's introduction of a new architecture called Account Aggregator (AA) could revolutionize the national credit landscape'. The ideas are in a nascent stage but it would be safe to say that both hold the potential to be game changers. And both the ideas are informed and inspired by the Aadhaar approach.

Awe and applause have followed successes. The Aadhaar approach has been lauded and recommended as the pathway to creating digital public infrastructure to transform economies and support inclusive growth. In a paper published in March 2023, the International Monetary Fund observes that 'India's foundational DPI, called India Stack, has been harnessed to foster innovation and competition, expand markets, close gaps in financial inclusion, boost government revenue collection and improve public expenditure efficiency.' It also suggests that 'India's journey in developing a world-class DPI highlights powerful lessons for other countries embarking on their own digital transformation, in particular a design approach that focuses on shared building blocks and supporting innovation across the ecosystem.' A recent UNDP report presented at the G20 Summit in September 2023 underlines the core characteristic of Aadhaar as one that 'establishes trust by democratising the foundational capability of authenticating that the individual is who they say they are'. It adds, 'Aadhaar is interoperable, built on open standards, and provides a sandbox environment for innovation, enabling public and private

Introduction

service providers (mobile network providers and financial institutions) to integrate their platforms. It is built on robust governance frameworks and its DPI characteristics enabled the country to make upgrades easily to respond to pockets of exclusion, as demands and needs change.' Bill Gates has frequently cited the Aadhaar success story as he has campaigned and championed the need for ID systems to 'make the world's invisible people, visible'.

The World Bank has cited Aadhaar and India's approach to digital public infrastructure – including Aadhaar and UPI – as a model for financial inclusion. At the recently concluded G20 Summit, the World Bank presented a report on policy recommendations for advancing financial inclusion and productivity gains through DPI. It says, 'The India Stack exemplifies this approach, combining digital ID, interoperable payments, a digital credentials ledger, and account aggregation. In just six years, it has achieved a remarkable 80% financial inclusion rate—a feat that would have taken nearly five decades without a DPI approach.' Indeed, the World Bank is now funding countries to create DPI frameworks in an effort to replicate the Indian success.

A host of countries have sought India's help to set up their digital public infrastructure. It bears mention that over 50 countries have tried and struggled to build national ID systems. The quest faces many challenges – choice of policy, technology, levels of interoperability, scale, sustainability, affordability and assurance of uniqueness. Naturally, countries have sought India's expertise. The UIDAI and the uniqueness of Aadhaar

Introduction

model is a strategic asset for India and the participation of UIDAI is ruled out. It is true that India has championed the cause of DPI to propel democratisation of technology for governance. Equally, it is also true that the government – given the political sensitivities enveloping data privacy – has stayed out of any involvement in design and implementation of DPI systems in other countries.

The quest of the aspiring countries is being enabled by the Indian ecosystem. A group of nongovernment entities, including Indian Software Product Industry Round Table (iSPIRIT), stepped in to create a unique entity called MOSIP – the Modular Open Source Identity Platform. The platform, anchored at the International Institute of Information Technology in Bengaluru, is funded by iSPIRIT and philanthropies, and is led by Prof S. Rajagopalan and an accomplished team of technologists.

The MOSIP team offers a modular system that is interoperable, scalable, inclusive and trusted. Very simply, countries can leverage the flexibility of the open source MOSIP model to customise, to build their own versions of Aadhaar. MOSIP has helped set up DPI in 11 countries – Morocco, Uganda, Ethiopia, Philippines, Sri Lanka, Madagascar, Niger, Burkina Faso, Sierra Leone, Guinea, Togo – with a combined population of 441 million. Its systems have recorded over 90 million registrations on the platforms. MOSIP has six national rollouts and five pilot projects up and running. The MOSIP collaboration brings on board an eco-system of over 80 providers of equipment and services. New MOUs have been signed with eight

Introduction

countries – such as Armenia, Suriname, Antigua, Barbados, Trinidad and Tobago, Papua New Guinea, and Mauritius. The Aadhaar revolution is now global.

It is true that ushering population scale solutions in any diverse political economy is challenging—more so in the world's largest democracy. Jean-Claude Juncker, former chief of the European Union, once said, 'We all know what to do, we just don't know how to get re-elected after we've done it.' The fact is transformative change arrives at the intersection of consultation and cooperation. Success demands public private collaboration. The Aadhaar experience illuminates that when civil society, politics and policy come together it is possible to engineer a revolution.

Preface

WHY AND WHY NOW

The challenge confronting leaders in the 21st century is less about what to do and more about how to get it done. Even when it is evident what needs to be done, how do you take an idea, a solution and navigate it through the warren of interests to make it happen. And, if possible, even get re-elected for your troubles. The truism about government is that what can go wrong will go wrong. In a democracy anyone, and everyone, has the right to obstruct, delay and detain progress.

This is particularly pertinent for the world's largest democracy. India's political economy is replete with tales of how things did not happen. The lament is preceded by the ubiquitous 'if only', about how solutions were thought of but the ideas did not translate into action. For the three decades and more that I have been writing about the issues that haunt India, my studies show that the reasons for failure are located in its structural and political complexities.

The fear of political blowback has engineered a strong

consensus for weak reforms. The volume of literature on India's policy shelves has solutions for all the ills; if deployed they would have delivered quantum change, transformed potential into promise. The crux of the matter is the absence of, and need for, a template for making a good idea happen, even where there is political legitimacy.

Electoral mandates are necessary but evidently not enough to propel change. The person at the helm, with her/his aura of power, is also not the only criterion as the person's capacity to navigate hurdles waxes and wanes with public events. Public enthusiasm, initially sold on the promise of a solution, comes with a sell-by date.

Political mandates matter, but delivering on promises requires institutions. And it takes individuals to build those institutions, so expertise matters, as does the system's openness to lateral induction of talent. For an idea to succeed, no matter how worthy on its own, all these elements must come together to form a unique constellation.

The genesis of this book can be traced to a breakfast meeting over couscous upma and coffee with Reuben Abraham, who likes to be called a 'pracademic' (practising academic). We were discussing whether a pattern can be distilled from success stories; if success can be replicated. Aadhaar was in the headlines and entered the conversation naturally. How did India build the world's largest identity platform at such frugal cost with such smart architecture in such a short time? How

Preface

did Nandan Nilekani, an 'outsider', and the band of techies and bureaucrats at UIDAI, engineer a platform for India's 12-digit revolution?

Conventional wisdom tells us that by studying the particular, it is possible to illuminate the general. The original idea was to put together a policy paper and a tool box for the IDFC Institute on how Nilekani and Team UIDAI built an institution to institute an idea. As I explored the back stories, the twist and turn of events, and the interplay of politics and personae, the policy paper developed into this biography of Aadhaar.

I have studied public policy and the political economy of post-Independence India, especially since the 1991 liberalisation. My interrogation of history, and coverage of every general election since 1984 and twenty-seven national budgets, throws up a constant. It reveals that, bar exceptions, any measurable change for the betterment of India's people is propelled only by a full-blown crisis. In stark contrast, the birth of Aadhaar seven years ago was a planned one, even if it now faces a crisis of sorts, of legal inadequacies and, therefore, of public faith.

As I studied its linear history, what stood out was that two national parties – with diametrically opposing ideologies – invested political capital in the programme to take it forward. The enrolments – 590 million during the Congress-led UPA and 560 million in the three years of the Bharatiya Janata Party-led National Democratic Alliance – represent a rare commonality of purpose. And Aadhaar has seen ups, downs and turnarounds under both regimes, with the idea itself morphing.

Preface

When it came to thinking about the title of this book, some aspects were obvious, like Aadhaar's history and the use of biometrics combined with a unique 12-digit number. The question that needed answering was this: is it a revolution in the making?

What is a revolution? As John Kenneth Galbraith said, all successful revolutions are the kicking in of a rotten door. The unique identity programme affords millions – particularly the marginalised – an instrument to state and prove 'I am who I am'. The fact is, for decades governments poured trillions of tax-payer rupees, nearly three per cent of GDP, towards subsidies, scholarships, pensions and other social programmes. Nearly half of it never reached the intended beneficiaries due to corruption. The enrolment of the 1,150 million persons for a unique identity number, so that beneficiaries could be identified, especially in India's systemic landscape pockmarked with incapacity, is globally unprecedented. Aadhaar's potential to empower and enable transformation is revolutionary.

Then came the narration. How should the Aadhaar story be told? There was the politics, the economics, the technology, the dichotomies, the concerns of a diverse society about data protection and privacy, differing views on whether Aadhaar is needed or is a non-essential. I decided to let the story tell itself.

Aadhaar is an ongoing revolution, warts and all. Clearly there are chinks, issues and infirmities, systemic gaps in accountability and protection of privacy, the

Preface

spectre of a surveillance state sending chills up collective spines. These concerns have been charted through the following chapters. The issues which yet need to be resolved, and the next steps, feature in the Epilogue.

The discourse in India is frequently a proxy war of politics and personalities. Of course democracy is messy and can be noisy. Dissent is healthy but a distinction must be made between the baby and the bathwater. The quest of this book, and the reason it is being written now, is to push the envelope of debate from what is not to what it must not be and what it must.

1
Who I Am

THE BIRTH OF AADHAAR AND THE NEED FOR IT

Identity is a complex question in any country. In India, that complexity is compounded by the political and economic panorama of a billion-plus population.

The tell-tale signs of identity are everywhere in India's colourful landscape – threads, marks on the forehead, amulets, tattoos, headgear and, indeed, dress. While these signs may signal belonging, identify the person in terms of caste, class and creed, they do not help in establishing individual identity. While context may indicate 'Who Am I' in terms of belonging, it does not establish 'Who I Am', rather, 'I am who I say I am'. Identity does not translate into identification.

For decades, India's political class has leveraged identity politics to win elections. However, promises did not translate into dividends as the instrument to establish individual identity was inadequate, even missing. Year after year, governments allocated trillions of rupees, nearly 3 per cent of GDP, towards subsidies, scholarships and pensions, on programmes to improve delivery of health services, and for education. Depending on the policy and the geography, nearly half of it never reached the intended beneficiaries because establishing individual identity was arduous.

That allocations were running down a bottomless sink-hole was known but, in 1985, the system was shocked awake by a tragic story that occupied the front pages of newspapers across the nation. That summer, Phanus, a destitute woman in Kalahandi in Orissa, unable to feed her family, sold her twelve-year-old sister-in-law for a mere Rs 40. The news triggered outrage. Rajiv Gandhi, who was then the prime minister of India, visited the area and was stunned at the level of deprivation he saw.[1]

Kalahandi had been in a state of perpetual famine. Two decades earlier, Indira Gandhi had made the same journey. Between her visit and that of her son, little had changed, indeed the situation had worsened.

On his return to Delhi, Rajiv Gandhi held a series of meetings and pushed the bureaucracy to find solutions. In 1986–87 India spent over Rs 37 billion in food and fertiliser subsidies, which was over 1.7 per cent of GDP, and over Rs 59 billion on social sectors, especially health and education.[2][3] Yet, very little of the money allocated under various schemes was reaching the intended beneficiaries. A few months later, Rajiv Gandhi toured Rajasthan. The story was not very different there, or in the other states he visited. Over 40 per cent of India's population was living below the poverty line.

The reality was grim. And Rajiv Gandhi put it succinctly: 'Out of Rs 100 allocated to an antipoverty project only Rs 15 reaches the people.'[4] The acronym-soup of programmes brewed in Delhi cost the government more and more but delivered little on the ground. The remainder, he said, was lost to administrative costs and gobbled up by middlemen, power brokers, contractors and the corrupt. Phanus and others like her, the poorest of the poor, were no better off.

This is best illustrated in the delivery of subsidised foodgrain ('ration', as it is commonly referred to), a critical intervention to alleviate poverty. The 'ration card' entitled beneficiaries to a quota of subsidised commodities which were affected by availability, particularly in the hinterland, and cost substantially more: basics like rice, wheat, edible oil, kerosene and sugar. After queuing up for hours, they had to go back with little – or nothing. Many who desperately needed help found themselves off the list and many who did not exist were on the list. Worse, theft was defined as leakage and distribution loss. The system was being gamed.

In 1985, the Planning Commission found that 'Beneficiary households were not drawing the ration even for one out of 11 commodities because of their irregular supply and poor quality.'[5] Between 1985 and 2004, six different studies, including by the World Bank and the Planning Commission, revealed that food grains did not reach beneficiaries and there was large-scale leakage. The government waddled along, with some tinkering and incremental changes. Food subsidy allocation increased from Rs 20 billion to over Rs 270 billion between 1986 and 2004.[6]

An evaluation by the Planning Commission in 2004 revealed that 'In 2003–04, 16 states were issued 14.07 metric tonnes of food grain of which only 5.93 metric tonnes reached BPL families'.[7] Nobody quite knew what happened to the rest. A Planning Commission Study, in 2005 said that 'about 58 per cent of the subsidised food grains issued from the Central Pool do not reach the BPL families because of identification errors, non-transparent operation and unethical practices' in what was designed as the Targeted Public Distribution System.[8] Indeed, in 2008, Montek Singh Ahluwalia, deputy chairman of the Planning Commission, revealed that only 16 paise out of a rupee was reaching the targeted poor.'[9]

The affliction was not limited to the public distribution system for foodgrain. Fuel subsidies – for kerosene and LPG and diesel – had shot up from Rs 62 billion in 2002 to Rs 760 billion in 2009. Subsidised kerosene was diverted for adulteration of fuels. LPG subsidy continued to be drawn even by dollar billionaires. Fertiliser subsidies created distortions in usage and were cornered by companies.

India muddled along. Two decades later, Rahul Gandhi was repeating what his father had said in 1987.[10] Post liberalisation, between 1991 and 2010, India's spend on subsidies for food, fuel and fertilisers shot up from Rs 122 billion to Rs 1.73 trillion, and allocations for the social sector, by Centre and states cumulatively, went up from Rs 102 billion to Rs 5.29 trillion.[11] Outlays, however, did not translate into outcomes.

Successive governments crafted public programmes for the needy but found benefits being cornered, if not captured, by the politically muscular. Persistent inflation created room for group entitlements and strident demands for higher allocations, turning subsidies into a hydra-headed monster. This had a multiplier effect across the political economy.

The intended beneficiaries of entitlements continued to struggle. Running from pillar to post, many were fleeced and had to pay 'under the table' (the quaint connotation for cash-corruption) for multiple official signatures and pieces of stamped paper to simply prove his, or her, individual identity. There were delays in the delivery of public services, denial of benefits, including wages and pensions, and diversion of public funds for private profit.

To establish that she, and he, actually existed in flesh and blood, to prove bonafide, the system needed an instrument to establish an individual's unique identity, one that could be used ubiquitously.

●

On a weekday, at the end of a day of meetings, Nilekani set up to meet with an old friend, K.P. Krishnan, over a meal. Whenever Nilekani was in Delhi, Krishnan and he would try and catch up for a relaxed meal, over which they would talk about issues, ideate on solutions.

Krishnan, then joint secretary in the Ministry of Finance (financial markets), had just returned from one of his meetings. That day it was the High Level Coordination Committee on Financial Markets, chaired by the Governor of the Reserve Bank of India (RBI) and attended by the who's who of financial markets.

The issue challenging officialdom was enforcement of customer due diligence by financial institutions. In simple English, the question was whether banks or others had a way of knowing whether the person they presumed to know was the person who he/she claimed to be. These days, the process has a fancy, frequently used acronym – KYC, know your customer.

On the flip side of this problem was the customer who had to suffer the 'triplicate' culture that ruled access to services. If someone wanted to open a bank account, he had to find an introducer and fill in a plethora of documents in triplicate. This was repeated every time and for every kind of service, from mutual funds to fixed deposits to bonds. Opening an account with a bank or a mutual fund was a trekking trip through red tape.

The diktat of the high-level committee to systemise the process was not necessarily driven by a desire to make life easier for the customer. It was propelled by a promise made in the Prevention of Money Laundering (PML) Act.

Who I Am

The Act, passed during the Atal Bihari Vajpayee regime and notified only three years later in 2005, explicitly states in its preamble the need to fulfil an international commitment, to combat money laundering by enforcing customer due diligence.[12]

Although India had made an express commitment way back in 1990 and then again in 1998, the imperative to legislate the PML Act stemmed from the fallout of the 11 September 2001 terrorist attacks in New York. Soon after 9/11, the world woke up to the fact that illicit funds had financed the terror attack. In a move to curb this, the US government revived the inter-governmental body, the Financial Action Task Force (FATF), which was established in 1989 but was comatose, to combat money laundering, terror financing and threats to the global financial architecture.

India needed to be on board the FATF, which set global standards for transactions. Crucial for success was a system of knowing the customer. India's case was, and has been, that its problems are complex and unique. And in a sense it did face a unique problem, of identification, of establishing a system that could denote and validate the identity of a person as claimed.

The political economy was littered with multiple systems of identification and identity cards – from ration card to driving licence to passport – each riddled with fakes and ghost entities. Some states had more ration cards than households.[13] [14] The systemic debility also precluded financial inclusion as nearly two-thirds of

Indians were out of the banking system, which impacted the efficacy of government programmes.

And then there was the issue of national security. In April 2000, following up on the Kargil Review Committee Report, the Vajpayee regime formed a Group of Ministers (GoM) led by L.K. Advani, which included George Fernandes, Jaswant Singh and Yashwant Sinha, to look into the various aspects of internal and external security. In February 2001, the GoM (assisted by four task forces) recommended a comprehensive systemic overhaul of the country's security and intelligence apparatus in keeping with the technological revolution.

One of the recommendations was to 'institute a multipurpose National Identity Card'. In the fifty-fourth year of the Republic, the Vajpayee regime amended the Citizenship Act and inserted a new section to enable the issue of 'National Identity Cards'.[15] This was tasked to the Ministry of Home Affairs under the National Population Register. A pilot was launched in April 2003, in thirteen states.

The first set of national identity cards under the 'pilot project on Multi-purpose National Identity Card (MNIC)' was handed over to the citizens of Pooth Khurd in Delhi's Narela area on 26 May 2007, by D.K. Sikri, then registrar general, India & registrar general of citizens registration.[16] The government told Rajya Sabha MP Rama Muni Reddy that the delay was due to 'complex process and technological issues'.[17]

India continued to be haunted by ghosts of the

past and present which refused to allow the birth of a unique identification for every individual. Solutions were wracked by a confounding circular challenge. To get a document you needed to prove identity and to prove identity you needed some document. This led to the creation of exclusion zones. Meanwhile, programmes involving thousands of crores of tax-payer money meant for the poor were subsidising the rich.

•

Over dinner that night Nilekani told Krishnan, 'All that is needed is to induct technology to establish that you, K.P. Krishnan, are K.P. Krishnan and issue a unique identity number that can be validated across the country.' Once this is established, the other factors will follow – whether it is customer due diligence or beneficiary due diligence. Krishnan agreed.

It was the mother of all solutions but easier said than done. The ground realities of India's politics being what they are, politicians thwarted the idea – particularly in states on the border where an individual's status – resident or citizen – is a political hot potato. The Multi-Purpose National Identity Card had a rocky start. It was started during Advani's tenure as home minister, it was seen as his idea, therefore tagged as a BJP project. The Bihar government, in 2003, then led by Rashtriya Janata Dal (RJD) with Rabri Devi as chief minister had refused to implement the ID card project.[18] RJD was now part of the United Progressive Alliance (UPA). Within the

Congress many of its members, particularly from Assam, had issues with the 'infiltrators' narrative. The MNIC project crawled on 'pilot' mode. The debate continued.

The kernel of thought stayed with Nilekani. In 2008, he expanded on the idea in his book, *Imagining India – Ideas for the New Century*. The book itself was born out of a romance with the idea of building new instruments for a modern state, after his involvement in promoting 'India Everywhere' at Davos in 2006. It was his view of India in the modern world, the social and systemic schisms, the challenges which he saw as opportunities for transformation.

Indians, he wrote, have a multitude of ways to identify themselves depending on when, with whom and where they interact with the state. This has created a plethora of systems and identification cards as the government, working in silos, deals with different sets of people to deliver different sets of services and goods.

Quite naturally, multiplicity has created a landscape of opportunity for evasion, diversion and fraud, and precluded people from securing goods, services and entitlements. The solution, Nilekani observed, was to leverage the power of technology, to create a national register of unique IDs and link it to the targeting and delivering of services, goods and entitlements.

The challenge, he said, was not in issuing smart cards but in building an intelligent infrastructure with a secure and scalable back end, a single record keeper for the whole country. 'An IT-enabled, accessible national ID system,' he said, 'would be nothing less than revolutionary in how we distribute state benefits and welfare handouts; I believe it would transform our politics.'

Many of those who Nilekani spoke with found the idea alluring. Those who had been in government felt it would enable efficiency and equity. Vijay Kelkar, former finance secretary, the go-to man for both the Vajpayee and the Manmohan Singh regimes, pointed out that direct transfer of benefits would deliver multiple outcomes. It would enable targeting of entitlements, deliver savings in government expenditure and propel financial inclusion in the complete sense of the phrase.

The need for creating an instrument for definitive identity had been echoing in the government for over two decades. There was the Seshan surge in 1993, when Chief Election Commissioner T.N. Seshan sought, via electoral identity cards, to establish the authenticity of each voter. There was also the MNIC project, which was driven by the urge to bolster internal and external security.

Thanks to political exigencies, ideas were there but not quite there, present but not effected. The voter ID card project was caught between political positions on who was — and how to identify — an illegal, a subject of multiple agitations and litigation. The multi-purpose card struggled to take off — again a combination of systemic faults and political design. On the face of it, everyone accepted the need for individual identification, but those who privately opposed it ensured that it was not pursued with any urgency. Poor implementation took care of the rest.

In May 2004, the Congress came to power with the Left Front riding shotgun. The formation of the UPA was predicated by adherence to the agreed National Common Minimum Programme (NCMP). The NCMP declared that 'All subsidies will be targeted sharply at the poor and the truly needy like small and marginal farmers, farm labour and urban poor. A detailed road map for accomplishing this will be unveiled in Parliament within 90 days.'[19]

The declaration was triggered by the political and economic repercussions on account of poor delivery on one side of the equation and rising costs of welfare programmes and subsidies on the other side. In March 2006, the government announced a grand plan, 'Unique ID for BPL Families', and tasked the Department of Information Technology in the Ministry of IT and Communications to get it implemented by the National Informatics Centre. The project was to be implemented within – hold your breath, drum rolls – twelve months.[20]

In July 2006, a processes committee in the Planning Commission was set up under Arvind Virmani, its principal adviser, for modification, updation, addition and deletion of data fields from the core database to be created under the UID for the BPL Families project.[21] A 'Strategic Vision on the UID Project' was prepared in consultation with Wipro as the technology consultant. The flyover fix, to overcome issues of enrolment and to kickstart creation of UID for BPL families, was to link it to the ready database of election rolls.

By August 2007, the processes committee, which included officials of seven departments, had held seven meetings and put up a proposal for the creation of the UID Authority. An executive order under the aegis of the Planning Commission declared that this move was meant to align and enable attainment of the goals of the XIth Plan. Among the members on the committee was the registrar general of India, who was involved with the multi-purpose identity card project. Inevitably the issue of who would do what, why and how – the matrix of turf control in government – came up.

The matter was duly referred to the prime minister to be taken up in the cabinet, which now involved the IT minister, who was from the Dravida Munnetra Kazhagam (DMK), the home minister, who was from the Congress and the deputy chairman of the Planning Commission, a technocrat. Prime Minister Manmohan Singh, recognising the complexity of issues, created an Empowered Group of Ministers (EGoM) on 4 December 2006, headed by the redoubtable Pranab Mukherjee, formerly the external affairs minister and, as of 25 July 2012, the thirteenth president of India. The EGoM included the IT and communications minister, the minister for law and justice, the minister for panchayati raj and the deputy chairman of the Planning Commission.

Pranab Mukherjee explains, 'Since UPA was a coalition government it required time and effort to evolve a consensus. Through patient deliberations, we ironed out the differences and increased the areas of convergence.' He adds, 'The UPA government had been working on improving arrangements to ensure that development deliverables reach the intended beneficiaries. I was convinced this project was necessary to achieve goal.'

The EGoM first met on 7 November 2007. It recognised the need for creating a database of identity for residents and the need for an institutional mechanism to own and maintain the database. In its second meeting on 28 January 2008, the EGoM decided to create a Unique Identification Authority of India (UIDAI) under the Planning Commission and that the collation of data would be jointly done by the National Population Register and UID. The third meeting, on 7 August 2008, saw the creation of a committee of secretaries to iron out legal and technical issues.

On 4 November 2008, the EGoM authorised the notification of UIDAI as an executive authority, with the proviso for grant of statutory status subsequently. It was decided that UIDAI would initially create a database using the electoral rolls and instruct agencies in government to standardise their own. UIDAI was to decide how it would build the database. Operationally, it was to be anchored in the Planning Commission, and a core team of ten, to be created, would put up a detailed proposal. Simultaneously, the EGoM gave the approval for states to create UID authorities. The deadline for the first UID to be made available: December 2009.

The decisions were not easy – particularly since the contesting ministry was the Home Ministry. The Home Ministry, housed in North Block on Raisina Hill, was and is still seen as a government within the government. And it was totally opposed to a body being created for collecting and securing a database on Indians.

A lesser politician would have found it tough to mobilise consensus in the face of such stiff opposition. But Mukherjee, who has had a ring-side view of history and power politics since the 1960s, is regarded across party lines as the encyclopaedic authority on government and Parliament with an institutional memory few dare contest.

He deconstructed the opposition of the Home Ministry by interpreting the legal position and the provisions of the Constitution. The ministry was tasked with the responsibility of collecting data on citizenship under the National Population Register. UIDAI, it was made clear, would be collecting and creating an identity database on residents – and that data could not be deployed for seeking or granting citizenship.

Mukherjee, leveraging his stature, crafted a consensus for the inception of UIDAI. On 22 January 2009, the cabinet secretary, following the decisions of the EGoM, considered a proposal by the Department of Information Technology. On 28 January, UIDAI was notified, to be housed and hosted by the Planning Commission. The fifty-two-page notification listed its responsibilities and organisational structure.[22]

The notification was marked to the secretary to the president of India, secretary to the vice-president of India, cabinet secretary, principal secretary to the PM, to the deputy chairman of the Planning Commission, all ministers and departments of the Government of India, chief secretaries of all the states and Union Territories, secretary general of the Lok Sabha and secretary general of the Rajya Sabha. It was clear from the notification, signed by Dr Subas Pani, secretary, Planning Commission, that a giant superstructure was to be erected in Delhi and across the states.

By February 2009, the UPA was in election mode. The Election Commission held a meeting with all parties on 9 February 2009 to fix a schedule for the general elections. On 2 March 2009, it announced the schedule for elections to the Fifteenth Lok Sabha. The idea of UIDAI was put on hold; its birth would have to await electoral coronation.

•

The text message was terse: Can you be in Delhi by 5 p.m. this evening? It was Friday, 22 May 2009. The Cabinet ministers, including Prime Minister Manmohan Singh, were to be sworn in that evening. The message was from Rahul Gandhi.

It was not an entirely unexpected message. Nilekani had received a call on 16 May, a few hours after the 2009 results were out. The Congress had won the polls, and a second term, with an improved seat count – up from 145 to 206. The political air was thick with ambition and optimism. It was not yet clear if the young scion of the Gandhi family would join the government. What was clear was that he had a major say in who would be inducted.

Like his father, Rahul Gandhi is invested in pet peeves and pet projects. One pet project was to fix the broken system of education. He had his theories – born out of interactions with Sam Pitroda, who chaired the ambitious Knowledge Commission, and his own experience as a member of the Parliamentary Standing Committee on Human Resource Development. He had concluded that education needed a whole new impetus, a thorough overhaul. He had come to believe that the system needed, to put it in millennial-speak, a 'person from another planet'.

Nilekani had known Rahul Gandhi since 2004, when he had visited Bengaluru during the S.M. Krishna regime, and expressed interest in knowing more about technology solutions for e-governance. In subsequent meetings, the discussions were always about governance. The ideas in Nilekani's book were a meeting point. Nilekani had also known Manmohan Singh for some time – first as member of the Knowledge Commission and later, when India was promoted as the fastest-growing free market democracy at Davos.

Nilekani had shared with the founders group at

Infosys the possibility that he might join the government. They were loath to let go but acknowledged that this was something he wanted to do – Nilekani recalls with fondness how 'one of them even called it a messiah complex' – and they wished him well. He kept a draft of his resignation for the board ready.

Seasoned politicos will confirm that it is not enough to be on the shortlist – physical presence needs to be aligned to the opportunity. Induction into a Congress government, and in coalitions, is frequently a last-minute call or cancellation – competing interests can invent a show cause at the eleventh hour. Typically, hopefuls and aspirants arrive in Delhi the day before, or at least on the morning of the big event – preferably at a location inside Delhi's Ring Road, preferably ready with a suitable outfit.

Nilekani, untutored in the rituals of Congress politics, was blissfully in Bengaluru. It was already brunch time. The logistics of getting on a flight and landing in Delhi in time appeared dim. His home in upscale Koramangala is not exactly near the airport, and there was the infamous Bengaluru traffic to contend with. He asked around for advice and chartered a flight. By then it was noon. He received another message. It was not happening.

While Rahul was keen, the core team of the Congress – essentially, Sonia Gandhi, Pranab Mukherjee, A.K. Antony and Ahmed Patel – was not confident about defending the lateral induction. Bringing in a non-MP who was yet to be a Congressman as the HRD minister was definitely too steep a political ask for Manmohan

Singh and even the Gandhis. Remember, the previous HRD minister was Arjun Singh – veteran Congressman from Madhya Pradesh, first elected in 1957, old warhorse, master of intrigue and a dyed-in-the-wool politician who had been a minister since 1963.

There was yet a window. Only nineteen ministers, including Manmohan Singh, had been sworn in and portfolios were yet to be allocated. The wrangling with allies had led to the postponement of the swearing in of the full contingent. The second round of induction saw fifty-nine ministers at different levels being sworn in. During that window, Manmohan Singh called Nilekani. He saw value in the idea of inducting a technocrat into government but the elbow room was limited. One option was to enter the government via the Planning Commission, as a member – a post that qualifies for minister of state status but does not afford room for executive action to get things done. Nilekani wanted to get things done.

He spoke with Manmohan Singh a week later. He had a second thought – the UIDAI project had been cleared; it afforded an opportunity to get into government and actually deliver change. Manmohan Singh had a similar thought. Recalling the interaction, Dr Singh explained, 'I had this idea to use technology to promote development. I thought, considering his work and the fame he had earned in the use of technology, it would be better if we inducted him into government for a project where his competency was well established.'

The induction through UIDAI got a positive response from Sonia Gandhi, Pranab Mukherjee and Rahul Gandhi. 'The logic,' Rahul Gandhi points out, 'is simple. I believe that there are certain projects which when handed over to an insider within government, can die on arrival. I knew Nandan, I knew what drove Nandan. I knew he was the guy that could pull it off.'

Nilekani wanted to be sure about the outcome. He brainstormed with his friends on whether the idea of enrolling a billion Indians was doable. He then asked his friend Krishnan whether his friends in the bureaucracy would let it be done. He met with and got the concurrence of Montek Singh Ahluwalia, deputy chairman of the Planning Commission. He then sought an appointment and met with the prime minister on 15 June. Manmohan Singh was leaving for Yekaterinburg in Russia, to attend the BRIC and SCO summits.[23] They met for around thirty minutes that Monday morning to finalise the terms of engagement.

Nilekani was well advised and had gone armed with a must-get list. He knew rank and hierarchy mattered and asked for cabinet rank.[24] He ensured he would report to the prime minister and that the announcement of his induction would be in his words – it was critical that he be 'invited' to join government. He asked for a special cabinet committee on UIDAI so decisions could be empowered and insulated. He got an assurance that the law bestowing statutory authority to the autonomous body would be prioritised. Manmohan Singh agreed on all counts. More importantly, he passed the baton of process to Ahluwalia, experienced in the art of skirting minefields.

Even as he was raring to get started, Nilekani learnt his first lesson before joining government: lie low. Say nothing, speak to no one, tell no one anything of any announcement until the announcement actually happens. This, after all, was the Government of India. What was about to happen as lateral induction was disruption, for politicos, for bureaucrats and for status quo-ists. Also, those seeking the chair offered to Nilekani might attempt an undoing.

He waited. On 25 June, the Government of India announced, 'The Cabinet today approved the creation of the position of Chairperson, Unique Identification Authority of India (UIDAI). The Prime Minister has invited Shri Nandan Nilekani, currently co-chairman, Infosys, to join the UIDAI as Chairperson in the rank of Cabinet Minister.'[25]

A week later, as if cued to the process, the Economic Survey disclosed data on rising cost of subsidies, vindicating the need for targeting of subsidies. The survey revealed that the 'share of Central Government expenditure on social services which was 10.46 per cent in 2003–04 had touched 19.46 per cent in 2009–10.[26] It also emphasised that the delivery of subsidies and services was wracked by leakages and urged a mechanism to address this.[27]

On 6 July, Pranab Mukherjee allocated Rs 1.2 billion

for the setting up of UIDAI. In his speech, the finance minister said, 'this project marks the beginning of an era where top private sector talent in India steps forward to take the responsibility for implementing the projects of vital national importance'.[28]

UIDAI was born.

2

Start Up in Sarkar

HOW TO GET GOING IN GOVERNMENT

Politicians tend to make grand declarations, and terming the lateral induction of private sector talent into government as 'a beginning of a new era' could well have been one of those. But Pranab Mukherjee is not given to hyperbole. After nearly five decades at the head table of national politics, he recognised the need for infusion of talent from outside – in the party and in government – and articulated it frequently. Mukherjee's evangelism, laudable though it may have been, is a tough intent to follow through, both for those inviting talent and those leaving the corporate world.

Logging out of the corporate world and into the government could have unintended and collateral consequences. On 9 July 2009, at 4 p.m., when the techies at Infosys logged out to attend the farewell party of one of the founders, Nilekani told his colleagues with candour, 'My only identity is Infosys. I leave to lead a programme which gives identity to every Indian. But today I am losing mine.'

His new identity would depend on the kind of identity he created for UIDAI. Between his meeting with Manmohan Singh and the announcement, Nilekani spent time consulting friends like Srikanth Nadhamuni, an engineer who had spent a decade and more in the Silicon Valley and ran e-Government Foundation, T. Koshy, who ran India's premier securities depository, the NSDL, and Sriram Raghavan of Comat Technologies, all of whom knew the challenges of inducting technology to improve the delivery of government services. He asked, 'Is registering a billion persons doable?' The answer was: yes.

Nilekani needed to find individuals to build the new institution. He needed people who knew government and who understood technology. Classical theory on governance lays much emphasis on the role of institutions in the development of the state. It is equally true that institutions are built by individuals. He had to choose his team from within the government – and quickly, so as to leverage the enthusiasm within the political system to be able to choose the right talent.

In government, whether it is hiring for a new programme or filling a routine vacancy, there is due process to follow. A list of probable candidates is compiled, including their curriculum vitae and confidential reports. These last are scarcely helpful – officers are usually graded as outstanding or very good without much detailing on the distinction. The exercise to find the right people demanded insight and inside knowledge. Nilekani sought out K.P. Krishnan, about whom it was said that he knew the civil list almost in its entirety. Krishnan suggested three names – for CEO, for CFO, and one for Nilekani to consider as private secretary (PS).

Nilekani first met with Ram Sewak Sharma. The postings held by Sharma, a 1978 batch IAS officer from the Jharkhand cadre, seemed straight out of a Bollywood script. He had been posted in the badlands where people and officers are frequently brutalised by political and other bandits. Sharma's hobby: writing code.

Sharma acquired his first computer in 1985, as District Magistrate (DM) of Begusarai, and a year later he introduced the district to a DCM 10-D computer and wrote a code to track down lost-and-found weapons. Later, as DM of Purnea, where he was looking after the treasury, Sharma wrote a code to enable a public grievance system. Then, as deputy commissioner at Dhanbad, he used it to manage elections. When he learnt that government personnel on election duty were co-opted by the political parties, Sharma deployed his code-writing skills to randomise the posting of people at booths. In 2000, at the age of forty-five, Sharma went to the University of California to acquire a Masters in, well, computer science.

At first look, Sharma is the quintessential bureaucrat, polite yet foreboding. Sharma says that he had been transferred nine times in seven years in Jharkhand. Luckily, for four of those years he had additional charge of information technology, so the experiments continued. He recalls his first meeting with Nilekani at the Maurya Sheraton hotel on 1 July vividly. 'I had heard of the new project. I knew it was going to be tech-driven. For me, it would have been another posting – one where I would work in an area of my interest.' He told Nilekani, 'If you have left everything to do this, have taken such a risk, I do not think there is any risk for me.' Sharma was concerned about work division. 'I asked him, how do we do this, and he was lucidly clear. He said, 'Ram Sewak, you will execute the project. I have to manage the ecosystem.'

The second person Nilekani met was M.S. Srikar, an IAS officer of the Karnataka cadre and a gold medallist from the National Law School of India. Srikar was doing the mandatory mid-career training at the IAS Academy in Mussoorie when he was told his name had been put up as private secretary to the chairman of UIDAI. He jumped at the opportunity to work in a new and unique project.

UIDAI now had a chairperson, a CEO, a PS. What it needed was that all-critical component of CFO, not just someone qualified to be a chief financial officer but one who understood the intricacies of oversight and accountability within the multi-layered systems that make up the government.

Enter Ganga K., liberal arts major and a technology

buff. Way back in 1989–90, as senior deputy accountant general in Chennai, Ganga had been involved in the computerisation of Provident Fund accounts in Tamil Nadu. Those days, the AG's office had vintage Ascota accounting machines, the ones with keyboards and the kind that add and print out a sheet to be stapled to the ledger. 'When the systems were changed,' she says, 'I was tasked with overseeing its implementation – it was quite an experience and converted me into a tech hobbyist.'

Ganga had just shifted to Shimla in May 2009, as the principal accountant general in Himachal Pradesh. She had heard about the UIDAI project. 'I was intrigued and fascinated but I didn't expect to be asked.' Then Krishnan called her and asked, 'Would you like to meet with Nilekani?' A week later Ganga drove down from the hills to meet the UIDAI chairman. Nilekani reviewed her CV in detail and asked her, 'Can you give five years to this project?' She said yes, 'with one caveat. I didn't want to be just the CFO. I wanted to be involved in the conceptualisation and implementation of the project.' Nilekani agreed instantly.

Between them, Sharma and Ganga provided Nilekani with a formidable combination. They understood technology and bureaucracy. They knew the punctuations that can free or freeze projects – the procedures, processes and pitfalls of operating in government. Old-timers will validate that allocation means nothing in government, merely a prayer, unless followed by sanctioned clearances, which is akin to the grant of a boon. Frequently, pilots and projects get stranded between these two points. The duo navigated the catacomb of words to ensure that UIDAI had, within weeks, the necessary powers to proceed and would not be held hostage to the clearance regime.

Others came to join this eclectic mix of talent and diversity. Ashok Pal Singh was deputy director general with India Post and dreamt of creating a bank account for every Indian. He met with Nilekani and Sharma to suggest how this could be done. He was invited to join and drive financial inclusion.[1]

B.B. Nanavati, an Indian Revenue Service officer armed with a huge cache of experience in IT procurement, was the author of many requests for proposals (RFPs). Rajesh Bansal, from the Reserve Bank of India, who was on a sabbatical at Duke University in the US, enabled perspective and understanding of regulatory challenges using his experience in designing digital payment systems.

There was no dearth of talent. Sharma says, 'People from different sectors from within the government and outside wanted to join the UIDAI.' Raj Mashruwala, a senior of Nilekani's from his IIT Bombay days and a serial entrepreneur in the US, wrote to congratulate him and came on to assist. Nadhamuni, who was one of the first people Nilekani had met and discussed the idea with, joined in to help.

Sanjay Swamy, CEO of mChek, wrote to Nilekani about possibilities and got invited to help with the mobile and micro payments push. Pramod Varma, an ex-Infosysian, one of the key finds of Nilekani and among the first five to jump in, was Chief Technology Architect and VP research at Sterling Commerce (now IBM). Varma brought with him expertise in architecture strategies for systems and joined as Chief Architect and Technology Adviser for UIDAI.

Viral Shah, a PhD in computer science and co-inventor of the Julia programming language for numerical computing, used for compilation, distribution and accuracy, worked on the design of the digital payment platform along with Singh and Bansal. Shankar Maruwada, founder of Marketics, with years of experience and insights into marketing and analytics, came in to drive brand building along with Shah and Naman Pugalia, a liberal arts graduate from Brandeis University and LSE who was interested in public policy. Govindraj Ethiraj took a break from television journalism to come on board as a volunteer, and so did Pawan Sachdeva, an investment banker.

•

The work and work space could not have been more typical of a start-up. The core team of UIDAI operated in two different geographies. The tech team and the private consultants initially operated out of Bengaluru from a makeshift office in a fourth-floor apartment in Palm Retreat Towers on Outer Ring Road, before moving into a proper office on Sarjapur Road. In Delhi, the team was squeezed cadre by jowl into a small office in the

Planning Commission building called Yojana Bhavan before eventually acquiring its own space in the Jeevan Bharati building at Connaught Place.

People in the UIDAI tapped friends in other offices to use their conference facilities, just to have some place to brainstorm. Vendors visiting the makeshift UIDAI office in Bengaluru doubted that it really was a Government of India project and also whether a national project could lift off from the apparent chaos. The Indian babudom, government officers, place enormous premium on markers: everything from the square foot count of office space to the number of phones to the towel on the chair is on the entitlement chart. At the Yojana Bhavan office, make do and make way were operating phrases. It didn't matter because those who were there wanted to be there. And talent, says Sharma, 'came squarely because of Nandan. He thinks ahead of time, he could draw talent.'

Those who wanted to 'contribute' sent emails and letters. Ganga went through over 200 emails and letters to assess level, capability, interest. Among applicants from within government were also those who aligned opportunity with geography. An Assam cadre officer from Karnataka wanted to be in Bengaluru. Another didn't want to miss his slot at empanelment, the process of being promoted to the next level in the civil service, but was looking for a Mumbai posting. An officer from Andhra Pradesh posted in the North-East wanted to be placed in Hyderabad. Ganga considered factors that would enhance work–life balance and sifted accordingly; largely, the pragmatic approach delivered.

UIDAI received thousands of letters and applications from a wide variety of people. The applicants were from across services within the government and from outside, and many were from the Indian diaspora. Techies from companies like HP, Oracle, Intel as well as non-techies applied. There were those who wanted to join, those who wanted to consult and young graduates who wanted an exciting internship. This public–private partnership of skill sets was important, and it was possible only because, even at the very beginning, the chairperson and the CEO had striven to enable a participatory framework, right down to laying down guidelines for volunteers.[2]

Nilekani had written to the National Association of Software and Service Companies to lend talent at their cost. Many came on sabbatical from their parent companies, many as volunteers – some were hosted as consultants to the National Institute of Smart Government, a body co-founded by Nasscom. Frequently, the Delhi–Bengaluru or Delhi–wherever flight tickets and hotel bills were parked on Nilekani's personal account.

There was no escaping the cultural conflicts. In the early days, the set-up was straight out of the sets of the Lucille Ball–Henry Fonda starrer *Yours, Mine and Ours*. Each brought their cheeky brood into the joint marital household, resulting in khatta-meetha clashes – the formal and self-knighted Sir brigade meeting the cool or, if you please, brash battalion. They had to consult and collaborate. Battles began, tussles ensued. Their differences stemmed mostly from context. Those from the private sector were taught to 'take risks to get rewards', like the annual bonus and upward mobility. Government, on the other hand, frowns on individualism, and inhibits risk-taking to preclude systemic shocks.

Shankar Maruwada remembers that there was a lot of tension in the initial days. 'There was a lot of judging of actions and words. Essentially it was about where you came from – the mindset matrix. For a lot of city slickers, government is not something one trusts. For bureaucrats, government is the only institution to trust. We think the corporate sector is transparent. Actually, the government is far more so – and that is how the checks and balances play out.' Both sides slowly came to terms with their different ways of working and a gradual blending of mindsets began.

The coming together of these creative minds produced sparks and many fires that had to be doused. Viral Shah provides a perspective. 'The objective was to improve the life of a billion people. Once you have a goal like that, you don't worry about the noise – and noise is a good thing in a democracy.' UIDAI pioneers remember the multitude of mind-scuffles and word-scrimmages but they are now reluctant to recount the blow-by-blows, perhaps because many of those creative combatants are now friends. The personal bonding between some officers and techies enabled back-channels to resolve tensions. Doubtless, the clash of ideas and approach among UIDAI's early titans continued, albeit a tad more amiably.

The chambers of the chairman and CEO were the epicentre, and the corridors the pathways of varying Richter-scale eruptions of the brainiacs. Sharma and Nilekani started laying bets with each other on how a particular issue or approach would play out. Ganga recalls with a smile that she would often be roped in to bear witness to their bets.

Says Sharma, 'Initially, there were a lot of tensions. I was seen as the leader of the sarkari-types and Nandan of the private-types.' The private-types would not think twice before shooting off a mail with a hunch, a wild idea, an opinion, to all and sundry. The sarkari-types used the preferred 'proper channels' route. The tension was not only about ideas or opinions but also the way work was to be organised.

One early sticking point was whether UIDAI should hold an open recruitment process or simply keep sourcing expertise. Nilekani, playing devil's advocate, triggered a discussion by asking, 'But is there enough talent in government?' Sharma responded, 'Whatever the faults of the system, it is an open system. I, a boy from a Hindi medium school in Uttar Pradesh, could make it only because the UPSC process, whatever its faults, was an open competitive process.' Sharma won this one, his being an ethical argument for equal opportunity.

Another deliberation was about procurement processes. The government is notorious for delays in procurement. 'UIDAI needs things yesterday,' said Nilekani. Ganga emphasised, 'All expenditure of public monies is open to scrutiny and [following proper procedure] is paramount.' Ganga assured Nilekani that the procurement would be designed to meet all time deadlines. The procurement processes of UIDAI, the use of in-house trials for cost and proof of concept studies for outcomes, outsourcing the man-machine matrix and opting to pay for services, are among shared best practices within the Government of India.

Through its approach to sourcing talent, UIDAI promoted the idea of diversity. Remember that in the government, the cadre (that is, the service and state an officer is attached to) is the reigning caste system. One of the things Sharma managed was to pull a diverse set of people together – an esoteric idea in government. As he now puts it, 'Creativity lies at the junction of different disciplines, not in a homogenous group but in heterogeneous groups.'

Within the officialdom, Sharma faced jibes about working for or under a private sector person. 'Guys would tell me privately, why are you helping a private guy? I simply said, we are working for the country. It is not that sarkari guys are all dumb or that private guys are all smart. Whosoever has competence has the competence. Rest is all stereotyping.'

●

The birth certificate of UIDAI, the notification issued by the cabinet secretary in January 2009, envisaged a project that was truly Leviathan. The objective of creating a unique identity was to be carried out by a large army of people. It had provided for thirty-five posts of Joint Secretaries for instance – even the Ministry of Home Affairs, the mother ship of the government, has only eighteen Joint Secretaries.

The structure of UIDAI, it would seem per the cabinet note, was patterned on the Election Commission. The Election Commission has a chief election commissioner, two commissioners, three officers designated as deputy commissioner, two officers as director general, around fourteen as secretary, seven as principal secretary, nine officials as director and nineteen as under secretary, besides other staff. Add to this another tier, the state election commissioners and the rungs of hierarchy that follow.

The UIDAI, however, was setting out to be different. The original template envisaged over 1,400 officers at different levels. Nilekani was looking at a compact superstructure, both nimble and efficient. He suggested to Ram Sewak Sharma that the number be trimmed to 200. Sharma, practised in pragmatism, simply said, 'Keep it to 300, all posts need not be filled.' Then, only half in jest, he added that there was no Bharat Ratna for restricting the size of an organisation.

Seat strength, a compact size, is one aspect of building an efficient organisation. What matters is not only what the institution and the individuals within choose to do but also what they choose to not do. The govern-by-maximum-numbers is, in large part, due to the do-everything-yourself approach which owes its genesis to the Mahalanobis era of planning. At that time, private capacity was limited. The model still holds strong because precedence is the divining rod in government. There is also the fear of risk-taking, and that lure of what can be personally and financially extracted while controlling the 'atmosphere' around assorted files.

The thinking within UIDAI was that success demanded it adopt the start-up approach. In the course of the first discussions and some robust debates, the core team concurred that the concepts, design and execution structure would be thought through in-house. Execution, as far as possible, would be outsourced, to leverage competitive market dynamics which could be incentivised. In short, the design template was 'in-house brains, outside limbs'.

Success demanded lucid articulation and simplification. The foremost task was to define how UIDAI would identify a person. What demographic data would be collected to define identity? The MNIC under the National Population Register listed sixteen fields: name, sex, father's name in full, mother's name in full, date of birth, place of birth, marital status, name of spouse in full, present residential address, permanent residential address, visible identification mark, finger biometrics, date of registration, date of issue, date of expiry and a photograph. Every card would carry a distinct number.[3]

During ongoing consultations, many departments in ministries wanted UIDAI to expand the data field.

They wanted data on blood group, disability, religion, ethnicity, income-related information, and so on and so forth. The tendency in governments, driven by the 'it may be useful' line of thinking, is to ask for and collect data that may or may not be necessarily germane to the objective. The operational logic is simple: if some agency is collecting data, add to the list. Of course, this frequently led to delays – after all, every entry required time and space and cost money – and could lead to denial as a large section of the most disadvantaged may not be able to answer/document all queries.

UIDAI wanted to keep the form as simple as possible and only ask for the relevant data for the purpose of identity. It was decided that name, age, gender and communication address were sufficient. Email and mobile numbers were optional as was father's or spouse's name. Following long discussions, on what must and must not be asked for, the format was ratified by the Demographic Data Standards and Verification Procedure Committee chaired by former Chief Vigilance Commissioner and Telecom & IT Secretary N. Vittal.

Identity needed to be validated – that X is indeed X or Y is indeed Y. And in a manner that is portable, readable and reliable. Nilekani articulates this lucidly. 'Today, Global Positioning Systems (GPS) enable us to answer the question Where Am I. The quest at UIDAI was that the system should be able to help an individual validate 'who I am' – rather, 'I am who I claim I am'. This required the capture of biometrics for registration.

Fingerprint identification was discovered by Scottish physician Henry Faulds, as a medical missionary to Japan in the 1880.[4,5] Faulds published a letter in *Nature* (28 Oct 1880) titled 'On the Skin-furrows of the Hand', relating how fingerprints were uniquely distinguishable and 'forever unchangeable' and conjectured its use for identification. The progress from use in forensics in Argentina to adoption by Scotland Yard to creation of an Automated Fingerprint Identification System took ninety years before its eventual adoption by the US Federal Bureau of Investigation (FBI) in 1970 – and featured soon after in *Diamonds Are Forever*, which was released in 1971.

In India, the capture of biometrics faced many a challenge. Expectedly, given the general nature of labour in India, a large number of people have bald fingers; they have no registrable or recognisable fingerprint. This was borne out in early trials. It was recognised that manual labourers – those working on farms and construction sites – could suffer exclusion and it was such people who needed valid identification the most. UIDAI's team decided on registration of all ten fingers.

Fingerprint biometrics was already being used in India. Indeed, a project called Bharatiya Automated Fingerprint Identification System, funded by the Department of Information Technology, was launched in January 2009. But the early adopters of biometrics technology were state governments. As early as in 2007, the government of Andhra Pradesh had rolled out

Smartcard-enabled payments with encoded fingerprint information for the Mahatma Gandhi National Rural Employment Guarantee Scheme (MGNREGS) and for Social Security Pension.[6] The Nitish Kumar regime in Bihar was using biometrics under the banner of e-shakti – to ensure correct and timely wage payment to beneficiaries in the rural employment guarantee scheme.[7]

The Central government was also using biometrics. A scheme to issue biometric cards to the fishermen of nine states had been rolled out in 2009.[8] Further, after the Mumbai terror attacks in 2008, the Home Ministry had decided to issue ID cards to those living in 3,331 coastal village across nine states.[9] The UIDAI team visited and reviewed the use of biometrics in existing programmes.[10]

The learnings from the reviews were brought into the report of the UIDAI Biometrics Standards Committee. To ensure reliability, a technical sub-group was formed to collect Indian fingerprints and analyse the quality. Over 250,000 fingerprints from 25,000 persons were sourced from Delhi, UP, Bihar and Odisha – nearly all from rural regions using different capture devices and through different operational processes. Analysis showed 'it was possible to obtain fingerprint quality as good as seen in developed countries, provided operational procedures were followed and good quality devices were used'. The report also cautioned that 'accuracy drops precipitously if attention is not given to operational processes'.

Nilekani and his team began looking at using fingerprints as well as iris scan recognition to boost reliability. The idea of iris scan recognition was comparatively new. The iris is described as a flat, coloured, ring-shaped membrane behind the cornea of the eye, with a circular opening in the centre that is adjustable; somewhat like a camera's aperture, it regulates the flow of light. The markers are colouration of the eye and structure. Although colour and structure are linked to genetics, patterns formed in the prenatal period make every individual iris distinct, thus enabling its use for recognition purposes.

It was in 1936 that Frank Burch, an ophthalmologist, first proposed using iris patterns to recognise individuals. For years thereafter, iris scanners made appearances in science fiction novels. The first iris recognition patent was filed in 1985 by Dr Leonard Florn and Dr Aran Safir, both ophthalmologists.[11] Florn met with Dr John Daugman at Harvard University to develop an algorithm for automated iris recognition.

The challenge in iris-based biometric identification is to develop a way to measure, encode and store the data for identification. Daugman developed an algorithm for exactly that purpose. In 1993, the US's Defense Nuclear Agency (now the Defense Special Weapons Agency) began tests for a prototype unit. On successful completion, Daugman was awarded a patent for his automated iris recognition algorithms in 1994 and the first commercial products became available by 1995.[12]

It was some time before iris recognition systems found their way into governance systems. UAE began using it

Start Up in Sarkar

in border controls in 2001, the US for field operations in 2002 and the UK for the aborted ID project in 2003. The technology captured the imagination of Hollywood scriptwriters and movie makers – Steven Spielberg deployed it in *Minority Report* and Marco Brambilla in *Demolition Man* – although tech pundits argue that the depictions are not entirely accurate. Apparently, you cannot use a dead man's eyes to cheat an iris scanner.

In 1984, photographer Steve McCurry had shot a picture of a young girl at a refugee camp in Pakistan. She came to be known the world over as the Afghan Girl.[13] The image haunted McCurry and many across the world for years. Eighteen years later, in 2002, he traced the girl to a remote part of Afghanistan and shot her pictures again. Her name, he learnt, was Sharbat Gula. But was she the same girl he had photographed in 1984? McCurry and *National Geographic* approached Daugman, who computed IrisCodes from both of her eyes as photographed in 1984 and in 2002 and identified Sharbat Gula as the original Afghan girl.[14]

The UIDAI team, after many trials, had come around to the view that it would use iris scans to bolster de-duplication accuracy. This was backed by a report of the UIDAI Committee on Biometrics chaired by Dr B.K. Gairola, the director general of the National Informatics Centre. Members included Dr C. Chandramauli, the registrar general of India, officers from RBI and the Rural Development Ministry, experts from IIT Bombay and IIT Kanpur, and two members from the UIDAI tech team. The committee observed, 'It is possible to improve de-duplication accuracy by incorporating iris. Accuracy as high as 99% for iris has been achieved using Western data.'[15]

The deliberations about whether iris scans should be included took over a month, during which time the UIDAI team listened to, understood and factored in issues with the technology. It was new and complex terrain. Raj Mashruwala stepped in and consulted experts. He met with Anil Jain, Distinguished Professor at Michigan State University and James Wayman, Professor of Biometric Identification Technology at the University of Kent – both experts and advisors to international governments. The UIDAI team also consulted Professor Arun Ross, Professor John Daugman and Professor Venu Govindraju[16] before finalising the design.

It was not an easy decision. Some of the experts they consulted warned Mashruwala and others that the iris technology would need enormous computing power and cost a lot of money. They were also told that inducting the technology may be easy but getting it to work in Indian conditions would be tough, even impossible. But Nilekani stood calmly resolute and the tech team overseeing biometrics was told, 'We have made a commitment, so there is no going back. Now we must find a way.'

The technology was still under patent and forbiddingly expensive. But serendipity intervened. The concept patent of Florn and Safir had expired in 2008 and the Daugman method patent was due to expire in 2011. In the course of discussions with Ganga and the finance team, Nilekani told them not to worry about the cost. 'Prices will drop and costs will come down.' Indeed, they did, and not just for iris scanners but also for fingerprint sensors as usage expanded – in India, Indonesia, Pakistan, Kenya, Germany and elsewhere.[17] Ganga believes that 'UIDAI disrupted the entire biometric devices ecosystem, prices for devices crashed.' It could be said that the economies of scale, the scale of adoption that leads to demand and supply, led to the fall in prices.[18] [19]

This well thought out punt delivered the reliability and assurance that the project demanded. The iris data provided a very powerful tool for authentication. Given that a large number of people were involved in manual labour and the authentication of fingerprints was tough, iris enabled inclusion of the poorest of the poor, by bringing down the margin of error to less than one per cent in the enrolment process. The process of de-duplication – using data to ascertain if the person was already enrolled – was considerably bolstered by the combination of demographic data, the ten fingerprints and iris data.

●

Each person who was registered needed to be given a number. If a billion people were to be given numbers, the number would need to be ten digits at least. Eleven digits would cover a population of 99 billion – remember, world population would only touch 11 billion after 2050. The UIDAI team decided they would go with a 12-digit number, and that the issue of numbers would be random – to preclude pattern and detection of gender, geography, ethnicity, religion, and so on.[20] The team also decided no number would ever be re-issued, even after the person's death.

The choice of this 12-digit format has a lot to do with modern computing. Technically, the identity number is chosen from eleven random digits. The twelfth digit is an instrument for detecting data entry errors. The system is similar to the one deployed in credit cards and uses what is called the Verhoeff Scheme. Since a billion and more IDs were to be issued, it was important to have a check-digit scheme that minimised data entry errors.[21]

The challenge of enrolment is best illustrated in the record-keeping of India's births and deaths. Every year there are an estimated 26 million births. To put that in perspective, the number is 2 million more than the population of Australia. Every year India witnesses around 9 million deaths, or roughly the populace of UAE. Technically, the system must record 35 million events – births and deaths. However, over 7 million events were not being recorded: only 82 per cent of births and 67 per cent of deaths were registered.[22]

Was there a database they could plug into and jump-start the project? There were many databases – ranging from PAN cards issued by the Income Tax Department to the ration card, from bank accounts to LPG accounts.

But there was really no database which had all of India's residents on it. Most databases were in different formats, many were incomplete, none were entirely dependable. Data was also corrupted by fakes and duplicates. In short, using any of it was fraught with risks. Data was also in different silos in various departments and states and in different languages. Even if they leveraged all the databases, it would be next to impossible to reformat them in any cogent or useful fashion.

It was clear that enrolment would need to be done from scratch. The core philosophy – think in-house and outsource execution – was to be their compass in imagining the process. So the team first arrived at what it would not do. Unlike the NPR, the UIDAI would not be issuing a card. The political system loves issuing cards – plastic, chip embedded – and that gets entangled in procurement red tape. More importantly, the cabinet note specified that UIDAI would issue identity numbers.

There were many discussions and heated debates on the subject among the UIDAI core team. Conventionally, enrolment is an in-house process. The Election Commission itself issues voter ID cards, the National Population Register issues national ID cards. Should UIDAI hitch a ride with the EC or NPR? Or would that limit target ambitions? There was the context and there was the circumstance of working within the government on this particular project. It needed to achieve scale at a rapid pace, it simultaneously needed to achieve a critical mass of enrolments so that the idea itself couldn't be killed.

Achieving the two goals demanded real-time innovation capabilities, quality assurance and solutions that could be monitored. This called for collaborations, partnerships, creation of platforms that could integrate solutions. Above all, the process would have to be usable without babysitters, even at the village-level enrolment centre. The core agenda of UIDAI was identification and the issue of numbers – essentially, delivering a service. This demanded being customer-facing. The process of enrolment had to be as simple as possible if they were to attain speed and scale.

The UIDAI team decided it would stay out of enrolment but would create the ecosystem. It would set out objectives, design the processes and outsource the work. It would create training modules and create competencies, and incentivise competition. It would leverage market dynamics.

The enrolment process was split in two parts. The resident could go to any registrar of choice – the processes were uniform – as per his/her convenience. The operator would collect the information from residents; take biometric impressions of ten fingers and scans of both the eyes. The data would be collected on software provided by UIDAI. The software would be coded for immediate encryption of all data, with a digital signature so no outsider could decrypt it – neither the operator, nor the enrolling agency, not even the registrar.

The second phase dealt with the back-end. The data packet, which is around 3 MB, is transmitted to the

Start Up in Sarkar

Central Identities Data Repository. The systems, software and architecture for CIDR were designed in-house and the operations outsourced. The back-end of the server uses multiple automatic biometric identification systems (ABIS) to authenticate whether the resident is unique – that he or she has never been issued a number till then.

The math of de-duplication that CIDR has to do is mind-boggling. The largest biometric database outside of India is US Visit (US Visa System). It handles around a 100 million identities. India's scale requirement is twelve times that, on account of its 1.2 billion plus population. The de-duplication process, Viral Shah points out, involves matching every fingerprint and iris scan with everyone who was already on the system. At a billion plus people, the math of the de-duplication process is complex. Shah offers to simplify it with a formula – $N \times N+1/2$. At a billion people, the system, it is estimated, would do 700 million billion biometric comparisons.[23] Following authentication, the resident would receive a letter at his communication address via India Post.

There were challenges on the technology side. The tech team had baked the processes, tried them on large samples – and the findings were placed in the public domain.[24] This was followed up with workshops for agents and device vendors and trials, learnings were wired for formulation of specifications for equipment to be used. Yet, in the real run, unexpected issues popped up. Take iris scans. The process of scanning itself is simple. The agent at the enrolment centre scans both eyes and the captured biometric is transferred via secure data lines to the servers in the CIDR. The servers at the back-end match the captured images with already registered ones and clear or reject them.

A few months into enrolment, it was discovered that a large number of iris scans were stumbling at the de-duplication stage, that is, when they were matched with existing scans to rule out duplication. The tech team was puzzled. Careful scrutiny of the position of tear ducts and eyelashes revealed that the images had been spun around. It seemed operators were scanning the eyes upside down, leading to the switching of left and right eye images.

Sanjay Jain, chief product manager of UIDAI, charged with ensuring end-to-end process and outcomes, recalls this as one of the many challenges. After much thought, the team concluded that the villain was the software that drives the device. 'The priority,' says Jain 'was to first halt the creation of errors. So the tech team wrote a patch for induction into the enrolment package.'

What were they to do with all the flipped scans? There was no question of going back to the field. Also, there was a lag between the enrolment and the arrival of the data at UIDAI for authentication – theoretically other flipped scans could be on the way. Jain says the tech team rolled up their sleeves to innovate in-situ and wrote software to enable flipping the iris scan for authentication. 'The tough call was the diagnosis,' says Jain. Fixing it was a matter of creativity.

The enrolment architecture borrowed liberally from the marketplace. Traditionally, governments opt for the capex model – that is, get allocations, push for procurement of capital equipment and execute. The UIDAI model was to incubate ideas and solutions, seek partnerships for operations and outsource process.

The architecture could be characterised as a hub-and-spoke system. The UIDAI was at the centre, the hub. The registrars were the spokes. The state governments entered into an MoU with UIDAI and signed up as the registrars. They, in turn, registered enrolment agencies. To streamline the process, a model RFP (request for proposal) for procurement of services was drafted and shared with the states to enable them to register enrolment agencies. The protocol for registration and enrolment was drafted by UIDAI. These agencies were required to go through training – everything from the setting up of enrolling stations down to the process of enrolment, and even the handling of grievances was written down.[25] UIDAI also had an online testing and certification platform for those wishing to take up enrolment.[26]

Nilekani says, 'We had an operator training process, training agencies to train operators. We created an online programme.[27] The UIDAI team trained over 150,000 persons. At the peak, over 50,000 stations were enrolling over 1.5 million a day.' UIDAI also entered into partnerships with institutions that dealt with a large number of consumers: the same hub and new spokes. It encouraged banks, insurance companies, municipal bodies, schools, post offices and panchayats to participate by offering premises to enable enrolment. Its tech savvy team also reached out to the masses in multiple languages, using online platforms like YouTube.

What about costs and funding? Via the state governments, UIDAI would pay the enrolment agencies Rs 50 per authenticated enrolment, which meant the payment was released only after the enrolment was de-duplicated at the CIDR and a number was issued. How did they arrive at this number? Ganga, who authored the process with Nanavati and others, explains the simplicity of the plan. 'We at the UIDAI had tested every piece in the process in-house to ascertain the cost and time factors. The math was based on trials and knowledge about what was required.' There was the device economics, which included computer, scanning device and sensors, printers and power back-up – an approved list of equipment was also shared with state governments and agencies. Then there was the software and the cost of manpower. The team did enough field trials to come up with a back-of-the-envelope calculation. For instance, it knew equipment costs would come up to around Rs 300,000 per enrolment counter.

The process itself was used to achieve reliability and cost efficiency. The enrolment package had embedded software that could tell the details of which enrolment agency, what time, where, which state, which centre, which city. UIDAI had all the metadata – the data that flowed out of CIDR told UIDAI who was to be paid how much, based on how many Aadhaar numbers were generated at the end of the month.

UIDAI paid the states Rs 50 per issue of number, regardless of what the states paid. Many states issued RFPs and got enrolment done at lower costs. That raised the question of what would be done to settle the accounts. It was eventually decided that the states would set up permanent enrolment centres and information centres with the money.

What set UIDAI apart and on the route to scale was the strategic departure from conventional practices, especially the outsourcing of processes. At an operational level, it limited the field of demographic data, it offered choice in when and where to enrol, it outsourced the registrar function to states, it created training modules and certification to enable private participation, it baked processes in-house to stipulate time and costs, it leveraged online facilities from training for the issue of numbers or updating of details.

Through it all, UIDAI retained total control over the outcome.

3

The Know Who Factor

KNOW HOW NEEDS POLITICAL AIR COVER

'Government,' Ronald Reagan, fortieth president of the United States of America, said, 'is like a baby's alimentary canal, with a healthy appetite at one end and no sense of responsibility at the other.' Reagan said this often, only half in jest, on campaign trails. His succinct summation of government-working aside, Reagan was eternally optimistic about the ability of people to solve problems, no matter the scale.[1]

Optimism, though, can at best be a prerequisite to getting things done in government. Even with the most gung-ho of a can-do attitude, it is not easy to translate intent into outcome. The private sector has a linear narrative, at the end of which is profit. Government has multiple storylines; this can result in competing compulsions. Such multiplicities of objective make processes and procedures complex. Succeeding in government demands patience, adaptability, a nimble approach.

The Know Who Factor

Above all, the doers need political air cover. The history of India's political economy is littered with pilot projects which were in mission mode but couldn't travel the distance because the ideas were not backed by political ballast. The ones that were backed politically, found visible success. The space programme led by Vikram Sarabhai and the Atomic Energy programme led by Homi Bhabha enjoyed complete autonomy and the support of the political establishment. The Milk Revolution had the heft of Sardar Patel, Jawaharlal Nehru, Indira Gandhi and Morarji Desai backing it. The Green Revolution came about because Lal Bahadur Shastri and, later, Indira Gandhi put their weight behind it. The C-Dot, STD and PCO-booth revolution – the latter brought long-distance telephone connectivity to rural India's fingertips – could take off because Rajiv Gandhi made it personal. History tells us that big ideas need the weight of the political establishment behind it, know-how needs know-who.

Nilekani says he knew of the criticality of political cover and had 'no illusions' or 'romantic notions'. In 1999, he had steered a citizen–corporate–government partnership programme called the Bangalore Agenda Task Force (BATF). S.M. Krishna was chief minister. The BATF, comprising some top names and talent of Bengaluru, worked in the bowels of government to try and redesign basic systems. Systemic support for BATF evaporated when Krishna exited government.

Political enthusiasm for ideas also comes with a

use-by date. In June 2005, the UPA government had constituted the Knowledge Commission with great fanfare. The Commission, headed by Sam Pitroda, was meant to create 'the second wave of institution building'. It was given the mandate 'to guide policy and direct reforms' in key areas: education, technology, agriculture, e-governance, to leverage India's demographic dividend.[2] By 2008, on account of a combination of turf battles, differences on reservations in education and waning political support, the Commission sank into oblivion.

The risk of losing political ballast is very real; UIDAI, too, had a limited window to build momentum. After putting in his papers at Infosys in 2009, Nilekani had sought an audience with, and advice from, Pranab Mukherjee. The then finance minister heard him out and issued a carte blanche – Nilekani could come to him whenever UIDAI faced a problem on the project.

Mukherjee is the quintessential man for all seasons, and has been throughout his political career. He can decipher legal punctuations as deftly as he can wrest resolution of political differences. Naturally, when UPA came to power, Mukherjee was the crisis manager for the party and the consensus builder within the Manmohan Singh government. By 2009, he had chaired over thirty GoMs set up to resolve issues that stemmed from the conflicts of coalition politics as also competing compulsions in a resource-starved economy. He was the head of GoMs on a range of issues, from airport privatisation to rural roads and from reservation for Dalits to Centre–state relations.

The Know Who Factor

A veteran of many regimes, he has had a ringside view of India's political economy since 1969 when he was hand-picked by Indira Gandhi to join the Indian National Congress as a Rajya Sabha member. As finance minister in the 1980s, Mukherjee opened up foreign investment by allowing NRI's to invest in India. In 1993, he steered negotiations at the Uruguay Round of General Agreement on Tariffs and Trade (GATT) for India's entry into the World Trade Organisation (WTO), arguing the case for opening up trade for export-led growth.[3] He carried the day despite stiff, opportunistic resistance from the Bharatiya Janata Party, and from within his own fractious party, the Indian National Congress.

Mukherjee says, 'In our country it is very important for reforms to be people-centric, especially for those on the margin. Acceptance and owning of the reform by members of the political establishment as well as civil society is critical.'

Mukherjee, more than most in the government, knew the magnitude of the challenge faced by UIDAI. He had heard the arguments and counter arguments, for and against the idea, through the EGoM that he chaired. He knew the turf battles that would ensue. He knew of the fiscal implications of rising government expenditure. He also recognised that, while the idea of unique identification would help target welfare, it would meet with resistance as political power brokers would be disempowered.

He had an uncanny comprehension of how hurdles

could either block or be adroitly moved aside. In 1980, soon after the Indira Gandhi government came into power, India faced a serious crisis – of poor funding and the broken state of infrastructure. Mukherjee was asked to head the Cabinet Committee on Infrastructure. He recalls, 'As the head of a cabinet committee, I was tasked with resolving both funding and execution issues of major infrastructure projects. I remember that the committee, uncharacteristically, worked like a corporate body. Our focus was on timely decisions and execution of projects in roads, ports and railways.'

This model was at the back of Mukherjee's mind. Soon after he had crafted the consensus at the EGoM, he met with Prime Minister Manmohan Singh and UPA Chairperson and President of the Congress party, Sonia Gandhi. He told them it was one thing to conceptualise an idea. It was quite a different challenge to implement it. He emphasised that 'the person we choose is very important'.

Mukherjee had clearly decided to champion the cause. He let it be known in his 2009 budget speech that 'This project is very close to my heart', making it clear to turf warriors that they would have to contend with him. The reason was simple. In his own words, 'I was not satisfied with merely letting it happen. I was determined to make it happen.'

The unique identity project had political air cover. It now needed to put in place structures to leverage it.

Nilekani officially joined UIDAI on 23 July, Sharma

a week later. It was, you could say, the coming together of yin and yang – one, the entrepreneurial man from the private sector, and the other pugnaciously insightful about everything sarkari. The duo immediately got down to the nuts and bolts of the project.

Building an institution like UIDAI from both the bottom-up and top-down requires information and insights; it also requires connectivity and demands networking skills. In a curious coincidence, Nilekani and Sharma were both IIT alumni. Sharma had done his MS in mathematics from IIT Kanpur in 1976 and Nilekani did electrical engineering from IIT Bombay in 1978. Indeed, many in the UIDAI team – experts, advisors, volunteers – were from the IITs. So were many of the civil servants connected with the day-to-day running of UIDAI. For instance, both of Manmohan Singh's private secretaries had studied at IIT – Indu Shekhar Chaturvedi at IIT Kanpur and Jaideep Sarkar at IIT Kharagpur. Manmohan Singh even referred to Chaturvedi and Sarkar in his 2010 convocation address at IIT Kanpur. 'Your institute,' he said, 'is well represented in my office too.'[4]

Historically, the exam and selection process for the civil services was loaded in favour of arts graduates. Although students of science could apply, and many did get into the IAS, they were daunted by the dominance of liberal arts subjects in the syllabus for the entrance exam. In 1979, following the recommendations of the Kothari Commission, the Union Public Service

Commission expanded the list to include science, medicine and engineering.[5] Since then, nearly four out of ten civil service entrants have been from engineering and medicine – many of them from IITs. As elsewhere, the old boys' network opens access in government too.

All said and done, implementation of ideas and enforceability of intent can be daunting. N.R. Narayana Murthy, one-time mentor and Nilekani's boss at Infosys, put it succinctly in an interview.[6] He said the political obstacles in a technology-driven project are always larger than computing ones. 'Technologically, it's a very simple project. The challenge is in making sure that literally hundreds of thousands of officers fall in line, they rally to his call and march to his tune.'

•

Action in government is demarcated by definitions of who can do what. It is also influenced by the structure of turf and rank – navigation requires knowledge, of all who can stall and stop process and progress. The UIDAI, unlike other government programmes, was yet to be backed by a statutory law. It was a creation of an executive order, housed inside the Planning Commission, which itself was the creation of a cabinet resolution of 1950.[7]

Conceptually the UIDAI was set up to generate identity numbers that would be deployed for delivery of public services and for targeting entitlements. These programmes were crafted, funded, monitored and delivered by a host of departments, each of which had a clearly demarcated turf. The unique identity project would impact at least a dozen departments and ministers. To structurally empower UIDAI, the Nilekani–Sharma duo suggested to the government that they create a mechanism for decisions to be blessed at the top. Manmohan Singh knew the sensitivities involved – he was heading a coalition regime – and understood the potential for political standoffs. On 3 August 2009, the government constituted a Cabinet Council under his chairmanship to advice UIDAI and 'ensure coordination between ministries, stakeholders and partners'.

The phrasing was important. So was the constitution of the committee. The Council comprised Finance Minister Pranab Mukherjee, Agriculture Minister Sharad Pawar, Home Minister P. Chidambaram, External Affairs Minister S.M. Krishna, Law Minister Veerappa Moily, Human Resources Development Minister Kapil Sibal, Rural Development Minister C.P. Joshi, Labour Minister Mallikarjun Kharge, Telecom Minister A. Raja, Planning Commission Deputy Chairman Montek Singh Ahluwalia and Nandan Nilekani.

The creation of the Council was in government-speak a message that the programme of unique identity had priority, that UIDAI had political blessings. The inclusion of the potentially affected was a way to assuage egos with the promise of consultation. It was declared that 'the Council will advise the UIDAI on the programme, methodology and implementation to ensure coordination between Ministries/Departments, Stakeholders and Partners. The Council will also identify specific milestones for early completion of the project.' The mechanism for speed and scalability had been set up.

At the first meeting of the PM's Council on UIDAI, held on 12 August 2009, Manmohan Singh emphasised that UIDAI was a 'high priority' project. He observed that 'lack of identity proof results in harassments and denial of services to the poor and marginalized' and also 'results in leakages'. Asserting that the programme would improve targeting and delivery, the PM urged the active participation of all departments at the states and the Centre. This meeting set the pace for the project. Mukherjee suggested that no time must be lost. It was agreed, in principle, to clear the UIDAI to register 100 million persons.

One hundred million persons translated into biometric data of a billion fingerprints and 200 million iris scans. That was more than any programme had accomplished at that time in the world. In terms of scale, 100 million would be ranked fourteenth on the list of countries in terms of population. It is, indeed, only in India that a project which involved registration of 100 million persons could be called a pilot project.

The first meeting also set the tone for the challenges that UIDAI would face. The meeting was attended by Mukherjee, Moily, Ahluwalia, Sibal, Joshi and bureaucrats from the other ministries listed on the Council. Home Minister P. Chidambaram, who was in

Chennai that morning, attending to party work, was not present. That evening, the registrar general of India and other officers briefed him about the meeting and raised a host of issues.

On 21 August, Chidambaram wrote to Nilekani. Regretting that he was not present on 12 August, he 'put down some thoughts on paper so that you may also reflect on the same. Perhaps, we could discuss these at the next meeting of the UIDAI Council.'[8] Chidambaram asserted that NPR was the most credible database and listed several points for discussion – on integrity of data, deficiencies in other databases (including electoral rolls), the authentication process, and whether enrolment would be mandatory or voluntary. The letter also raised the question of access to the UIDAI database on grounds of national security.

The point was one of control. The RGI's case was that UIDAI would simply issue unique numbers and maintain the database.[9] The RGI would have complete authority over the process, and would set standards for compilation and digitisation, and UIDAI could suggest modifications. The task of UIDAI was to assign numbers and ensure that biometrics and photographs confirmed to standards.

Chidambaram also wrote to the prime minister with a copy of his letter to UIDAI, requesting that 'these issues may be discussed and resolved at the next meeting of the Council'. A copy of the letter was marked to the deputy chairman of the Planning Commission, the host of

UIDAI. On 24 August, Ahluwalia forwarded the same to Nilekani with a tongue-in-cheek noting, 'I presume you are "seized" of the matter as GOI lingo would put it.'[10]

The conflict stemmed from interpretation. The EGoM headed by Mukherjee had stated that UIDAI's brief was to create the initial database from electoral rolls and the like. It also allowed UIDAI to issue instructions on standardisation to agencies that undertake creation of databases. Critically, it allowed UIDAI to 'take its own decision as to how to build the database'. The Home Ministry saw UIDAI merely as a BPO operation, like the tech project management units that assist on government projects. UIDAI interpreted the statement that 'UIDAI would take its own decision' as an assurance of autonomy.

The news of a tussle found its way into the media. The resultant speculation occupied attention for weeks. The issue mattered, for it related to the status of the Home Ministry in the overall picture. No matter which era, the Home Ministry has always been a powerful ministry. It enjoys a special status given that it oversees internal security and is tasked with ensuring political stability in states. It has a say in clearances, appointments, and in creation of institutions across the country. Pertinently, post 26/11, the ministry was seen to be more assertive on issues relevant to national security concerns. And P. Chidambaram, a combative and capable minister, one of the three most powerful persons in government, was at the helm. Deceptively soft-spoken and sharp,

The Know Who Factor

Chidambaram is obsessive about process and protocol, and he was now looking at an issue of due process. He raised all the flags.

On the other hand, in the UIDAI corner was Mukherjee, whose support was openly stated. Number two in the cabinet, Mukherjee was, in terms of de facto political standing, senior even to the prime minister. Earlier, as finance minister, he had signed the letter appointing Manmohan Singh as Governor of the Reserve Bank of India. Clearly a stand-off between two ministries and two senior ministers was a serious issue. Manmohan Singh recalls the confrontation of ministries and says, 'I saw I needed to bring consensus on this forward looking idea. The confrontation between ministries was a matter that had to be handled delicately.' The matter of who, what, how and when was referred back to the Prime Minister's Council, which, on 22 October 2009, was recast as the Cabinet Committee on UIDAI.

As the mandarins exchanged mails and letters, Mukherjee intervened decisively. In November 2009, he cleared Phase I with an allocation of Rs 1,473 million and ensured that the Standing Finance Committee and Cabinet Committee stamped their approval.

The UIDAI team revved up its presentation and consultation process. Among the early meetings was one at Shimla's Rashtrapati Nivas, once the Vice Regal Lodge and the winter retreat of Viceroys, now the campus of the Indian Institute of Advanced Study. In this October 30–31 gathering, Professor Peter DeSouza of the Centre for the Study of Developing Societies, said UID might be 'on the threshold of something significant and revolutionary' which could be 'transformational for India'. Professors Zoya Hasan of JNU, Sanjay Palshikar of the University of Hyderabad and R. Ramkumar of TISS, voiced their concerns about loss of privacy and the impact on civil liberty. Nilekani, Sharma and Ajay Mehta, of the National Foundation of India, presented the pro-poor emphasis of the project and countered theories of hidden agendas.

In the next few months, the outreach team sought and met with a broad range of civil society groups. These included the Indo Global Social Service Society in Delhi, SEWA at Ahmedabad, NGO groups from the north-east states, the Bodoland Territorial Council at Kokrajhar in Assam, civil society organisations under the banner of Econet, AFARM and National Centre for Advocacy Studies in Pune. Interested groups who wanted to invite the UIDAI team could write to them at a web address – and many did, like the students and faculty of Guwahati University.

The consultations thereafter expanded not just across states but also special interest groups, including those representing interests of Dalits, tribals, the elderly, the differently abled and those working in the fields of education, health, women and children. The UIDAI team created special modules of communication, and literature that included frequently asked questions and notes for the speakers. The conversations that followed presentations highlighted meta questions about the dilemmas of framing public policy. And also of social and economic liberties versus political liberties, the trade-off between benefits of UID versus loss of privacy, of trust and mistrust, from anonymous delivery of public services to identification for reaching the unreached, asymmetry of information available and of communication by the government. In a nutshell, questions that would continue to haunt the programme.

The operating model of UIDAI required the team to collaborate with ministries in Delhi and those in state capitals. This meant meetings which, as per government protocol, adhere to a set hierarchy – those placed lower in the rungs call on those above them. The UIDAI team didn't subscribe to this protocol. Nilekani, although holding the rank of cabinet minister, would call on ministers in the Central government and chief ministers and heads of departments and public enterprises. He had experience pounding the beat for business while in Infosys. 'I had no hang ups going to any office, I made sure they understood I needed their cooperation.' The practice was of strategic value. In government, there is an asymmetry of information. Meeting everyone on their turf afforded a holistic view of the landscape and more importantly, valuable information and insights.

Nilekani's meetings had begun as early as 29 July 2009 and were with potential collaborators – Ministries of Petroleum, Labour, External Affairs, the Department of Income Tax, LIC, Insurance Regulatory and Development Authority, the Indian Banks Association, micro-finance institutions, Nasscom and venture capitalists. The idea was to secure a buy-in for the idea of unique identity, source partnerships, understand the regulatory issues, and the depth and width of their databases – of LPG consumers, EPF accounts, passports and tax payers.

Meetings were also held with institutions – the Planning Commission, the 13th Finance Commission,[11] the Prime Minister's Economic Advisory Council, the Reserve Bank of India, the Forward Markets Commission, the chief accountant general, the chief vigilance commissioner, the chief information commissioner and the chief vigilance commissioner – to elicit views on government expenditure, transparency and anti-corruption initiatives. Between August 2009 and February 2010, Nilekani and Sharma had meetings with chief ministers and/or senior officials of Meghalaya, Karnataka, Delhi, Kerala, Tamil Nadu, Rajasthan, Uttarakhand, Goa, Gujarat, Andhra Pradesh, Himachal Pradesh, Madhya Pradesh, Uttar Pradesh, Bihar, Manipur, Maharashtra, Haryana, Punjab, Odisha, Jharkhand, Jammu and Kashmir and Chhattisgarh. The agenda was simple: to share with the chief ministers and the bureaucracy the rough contours of the unique identity project and solicit ideas and suggestions.

The contours of the project were now observable. UIDAI found its way into Mukherjee's budget speech once again on 26 February 2010. To appreciate the 'mention', one must remember that nearly every ministry and over fifty departments send in notes about their programmes to the office of the finance minister. Only a few make it to the text of the speech. Finance Minister Mukherjee said, 'I am happy to report that the Authority has been constituted and it will be able to meet its commitments of issuing the first set of UID numbers in the coming year. It would provide an effective platform for financial inclusion and targeted subsidy payments. Since the UIDAI will now get into the operational phase, I am allocating Rs 19 billion to the Authority for 2010–11.' It signalled Mukherjee's continued faith in the individuals and the institution of UIDAI.

As it happened, UIDAI featured in every budget speech by Finance Minister Mukherjee between 2009 and 2012.

•

The unique identity project had a problem of identification and identity, though: its own.

The acronym UIDAI was not an easy handle to work with. Governments typically fit in everything they want to achieve into a programme's title and then shrink wrap it in an acronym. They are beaten into pronounceability as files travel ministry to ministry, and acquire currency over the years. The Rural Development Ministry, for instance, has DIKSHA, NRuM, PMAY, NRLM, DAY-NRLM, MGNREGS, the last of which is Mahatma

Gandhi National Rural Employment Guarantee Scheme but is pronounced as Emen-REGS or ManRayGa.

The Unique Identity Development Authority of India, aka UIDAI, needed an identifiable moniker. It needed a name that would define the idea, which would be easily understood across India's thirty states and union territories, that would signify aspiration and deliver branding to the project. And be pronounceable. At one of the strategy meetings in late 2009, it was decided that, along with a name, the project needed an easily identifiable logo.

Many names were thought of. The private sector guys came up with names like Pragati Number, Unnati Number, Vishist Number, Sewank Number, Mera Number. Those from the government, used as they were to acronym-driven handles, came up with VIP Number. Others said, why not UID number, it is already in currency. There is also a vague recall that Aadhaar was one of the suggestions. The namkaran (naming) file was getting thicker. Adding to it in full measure was Ram Sewak Sharma, who every now and then appeared to have a burst of inspiration and reeled out options.

In the meantime, a team of UIDAI, which was working on communication and marketing of the programme, were out surveying for inputs. They were trying to understand common needs and social norms so as to create a push factor for enrolment. And several of those crisscrossing the countryside were restless,

The Know Who Factor

curious and passionate youngsters who had come in as volunteers. One of them was Naman Pugalia.

After graduation, Naman was at the crossroads of a decision: to join a financial outfit where he had interned or to follow his passion for public policy. He decided to backpack across India, mainly by public transport, to 'see for myself' and 'study the implementation of welfare projects' across the states. As Pugalia puts it, 'Being young and curious is a passport to knowledge in India, if you are willing to rough it out.' He would quiz local journalists, visit educational institutions, meet with officials and talk to people in rural India. It was his version of the widely regarded television series 'Bharat Ek Khoj', his very own discovery of India.

Sometime in July 2009, Pugalia, back at home to hit the reset button, met with Viral Shah, who suggested he join UIDAI. Pugalia had, as a matter of fact, already written to Nilekani, and he accepted Shah's offer with alacrity. He couldn't wait to decode the rest of real India, this time from the inside, as part of a focus group. One of the tasks of the focus groups was to explain the concept of unique identity, seek views and understand mindsets. Pugalia travelled across Rajasthan, meeting folks from academia, government and civil society. The issue of identity had resonance among rural people. Rajasthan has a high level of intra-state migration, labour moving around for seasonal jobs.

In Udaipur, Pugalia met with Rajeev Khandelwal of Aajeevika, a not-for-profit organisation that assists in documentation for migrant labourers. They also spoke about nomadic tribes and Pugalia decided to set out and meet some. He reached Mogiyathana, an off-the-grid settlement near Udaipur, nearly 10 km from any habitation.

The standard procedure was to collect a group, mostly men since women rarely participated, and have a comfortable chat. Around twenty elderly members of the Mogiya tribe sat down for the discussion, asking many questions about process and utility. It was a routine exercise for Pugalia, who had done several by then. Except for what happened at the end. An elderly Mogiya, Naiya Ram Rathore, put his hand on Pugalia's shoulder to tell him this was a good idea. And then he added, *'Agar aap isko vaastavikta mein tabdeel kar sakte hain toh bahut achha hoga. Pehchaan hi toh jeevan ka aadhaar hai.'* (If this idea can be translated into reality, that would be very good. Identity is, after all, the foundation of life.)

Naman Pugalia was so struck by the elderly nomad's statement that he drove through Rajasthan's desert dust till he found a cell-phone tower and connectivity. He called Shankar Maruwada, who steered the marketing and branding push, and told him about it. 'Aadhaar,' he said, *'Pehchaan hi jeevan ka aadhaar hai.'* Maruwada recalls that moment, and being instantly in sync with the idea. 'Aadhaar. Identity is the foundation, the very basis, of life.' He telephoned Nandan Nilekani.

Aadhaar it was.

The Know Who Factor

Aadhaar, it turned out, was almost an instant hit. It translated into everything that aligned with the idea and the utility of the identity project. It meant foundation. It meant the same in most languages and therefore enabled branding and communication. It conveyed the essence of the Aadhaar-wallah programme – a clear recognition of identity was the foundation for rights and entitlements, indeed progress and prosperity.

Next, Aadhaar needed an easily identifiable logo. It was decided that the logo would be crowdsourced. In February 2010, UIDAI launched a nationwide logo competition for Aadhaar. The parameters were clearly defined: the logo should bring out the essence of UIDAI, it should communicate that the number is a transformational opportunity for individuals and would equalise access to services and resources for the poor, and it should be easily understood across the country.

In the following weeks, over 2,000 entries were received from across the country. These were evaluated by a jury – the Awareness and Communication Strategy Advisory Council, comprising communication experts who were advising UIDAI. The finalists included Michael Foley, Saffron Brand Consultants, Sudhir John Horo, Jayanth Jain and Mahendra Kumar. The winning entry was by Atul S. Pande, who recalls that he hadn't even known about the competition; it was his sister who heard about it and urged him to enter. When he received his cheque of Rs 100,000, Pande, a designer by profession, said, 'I read through their concept notes and knew that

I had to create something which is easily recognisable. Any rural person would be able to can recognise the sun and the fingerprint.'

The jury that finalised Pande's logo said, 'a sun in red and yellow, with a fingerprint traced across, effectively communicates the vision for Aadhaar. It represents the dawn of equal opportunity for each individual, a dawn that emerges from the unique identity that the number guarantees for each individual.' It was decided that the logo and name would be unveiled at a public function. The question was, who should they ask to do the unveiling? The focus groups had come across many individuals in rural India who liked the idea and wanted to help. One of them was Dhaneshwar Ram, a school teacher from Azamgarh in Uttar Pradesh, who had met with a focus group led by Pugalia. He had told the group, 'this programme must succeed', and wished to contribute.

On 26 April, Dhaneshwar Ram unveiled the Aadhaar logo, spoke about his hardships to secure his job as a teacher and why Aadhaar was a good idea. Now UIDAI had a name, a logo. It also had a strategy paper – the 'UIDAI Strategy Overview – Creating a unique identity number for every resident in India'. The forty-five-page document listed every aspect of the project – the approach, the implementation model, enrolment process, authentication, data security, legal issues, technology architecture, project risks, and the possibilities of deploying the platform to extend and expand the use of Aadhaar.

But just before this strategy document could be unveiled, there cropped up an unresolved problem between UIDAI and the political establishment.

The establishment wanted a card, an Aadhaar card.

•

UIDAI had declared, right at the start, that it would only issue unique identity numbers. Nilekani had consistently told every audience, including the Cabinet Committee on UIDAI, that there would be no cards. The official printout with the unique number, reaching each successful applicant through India Post, would suffice. Yet, systemic pressure for a card had been mounting from both the bureaucracy and politicians.

Political parties, when they promise something to the electorate, want to be able to transact, issue something. This has created its own two-way street, with the electorate expecting something that can be instantly flashed, displayed. You see this in the endless photo opportunities at the launch of schemes – the backdrop, the bunting, somebody from the regime handing over to a constituent, amidst a sea of expectant faces, an object that is visible.

Ram Sewak Sharma, seasoned bureaucrat and therefore spotter of the politician's need-to-show compulsions, convinced Nilekani to agree to a card so that the project could move forward. The strategy paper thus added, 'UIDAI will issue a number. This number may be printed on the document/card that is issued by the Registrar.' A solution that reflected real-time accommodative innovation in policy.

The Manmohan Singh government, meanwhile, was nudging state governments. At a conference of chief secretaries – the head priests of the bureaucracy at state capitals – states were asked to set up cabinet committees under the chief minister to enable creation of the apparatus necessary for UIDAI to start the enrolment process. Simultaneously, the Union Cabinet approved a scheme for enrolment of Indian residents under the National Population Register of the Home Ministry and allocated Rs 35.39 billion. The NPR database was to be shared with UIDAI for biometric de-duplication and for adding the Aadhaar number.

On 1 June 2010, at the first anniversary of UPA II, Manmohan Singh expressed the hope that 'the first set of Aadhaar numbers will be issued soon – between August 2010 and February 2011'. He also added that 'the project will provide a platform for direct transfer of benefits and subsidies to the poor and will be an important instrument to expand financial inclusion'. An inter-ministerial group had already formed a sub-group to prepare a framework using payment gateways and mobile phones.

The buzz about Aadhaar had generated much enthusiasm among people. Many wrote to the prime minister. Madhukar Rao Choudhary, formerly speaker of the Maharashtra Assembly, forwarded a proposal by G.D. Patil, from Dhule in Maharashtra, titled JaiBharati Yojana and built on the idea of unique identity. Two

The Know Who Factor

final-year students of an engineering college in Tirupur in Tamil Nadu sent a twenty-one-page project report for a Personal Identification Card that incorporated biometrics and smart card features. These ideas were circulated within UIDAI and in government.

UIDAI had meanwhile finalised the technology solutions, released the list of empanelled enrolment agencies, signed MoUs with early enrolment states, signed up institutional partners, entered into an agreement with India Post to deliver the Aadhaar numbers. On 22 July, the Cabinet Committee on UIDAI approved the commencement of Phase II of the UIDAI scheme and allocated Rs 30.23 billion to cover recurring establishment costs and for project-related non-recurring expenditure. The government declared that the 'first set of 100 million UID numbers were to be issued between August 2010 and March 2011 and thereafter 600 million Aadhaar numbers would be issued in the next three years'.[12] Eventually it would cover all residents of India.

The system was gearing up for a launch. Just before it could happen, National Advisory Council (NAC) members raised the flag of disagreement and disquiet and launched a broadside against Aadhaar. The NAC, with Sonia Gandhi as chairperson, was a political innovation that enabled the Congress chief to exercise influence over policy while allowing activists to have their say. Economist Jean Dreze, member Aruna Roy and others raised questions about the haste with which the UID project was being implemented. Concerns were raised about the creation of a 'deep state' and disregard of democratic conventions. There was a call for a debate on the relationship between the state and the people.

In the 24 July 2010 issue of the *Economic and Political Weekly*, legal scholar Usha Ramanathan wrote, 'India's unique identification number project has been sold on the promise that it will make every citizen, the poor in particular, visible to the State. But the UID project raises crucial issues relating to profiling, tracking and surveillance, and it may well facilitate a dramatic change in the relationship between the State and the people. The Unique Identification Authority of India has not acknowledged these concerns so far.'[13]

Another group wrote an open letter asking why India was pursuing something that had been rejected by countries like Britain. One letter writer even congratulated Sonia Gandhi for disapproving of the UIDAI project. The activists were concerned that demographic data being collected could be used for profiling on the basis of religion, caste, tribe, language, income and political persuasion, and deployed for denial of entitlements and services. These issues had come up earlier too at meetings, particularly at one convened in May 2010 with NGOs, human rights groups and activists, attended by thirty-odd representatives of civil society. The issues flagged included accountability of UIDAI, transparency, exclusion of the marginalised, pitfalls of technology, efficiency in data capture, need for an ombudsman and, of course, concerns about privacy and data protection.[14] The UIDAI team had addressed these questions on multiple occasions, but the call to halt Aadhaar grew louder.

Manmohan Singh was unsurprised by the intensity of the opposition, the statements and open letters in the media, having experienced multi-pronged attacks since 2004. He was, at the time, facing the ire of activists over the handling of Maoist-affected districts and the Home Ministry's recover-ground strategy to combat left-wing extremism. His office advised Nilekani to pull back a bit. Accordingly, Nilekani – as the running quarterback of the programme between his team and the political regime – postponed his presentation to the NAC, which was scheduled for 30 August.

Ominous clouds of uncertainty were hovering over not only the launch programme, which was only a month away, but the UIDAI project itself. At stake were the assurances made by Manmohan Singh and Rahul Gandhi when they brought the UIDAI chief into government. Manmohan Singh and Pranab Mukherjee got into firefighting mode. The key was to convince Sonia Gandhi.

Rahul Gandhi stepped in. He told Nilekani to go ahead with the plans for the launch, and spoke to Ashok Chavan, then Maharashtra chief minister, telling him to prepare for the launch. Rahul Gandhi, like Mukherjee and Manmohan Singh, continues to be a believer in the idea of unique identity. He does not shy away from admitting to that critical intervention. 'I did back Nilekani then and at other times.' He was convinced about the efficiency of delivery and financial savings that Aadhaar promised, but there is more to it, he says. 'The identity of an Indian in a rural area is through his intimate network, through his community. India is urbanizing rapidly. When he/she moves from rural to urban, his/her identity, and therefore their ability to demand their rights and entitlements, gets messed up. Aadhaar is critical for change as it provides a foundation for the individual, which moves with him/her.' Aadhaar, the Congress vice-president is clear, provides a beachhead for the individual to defend her, and his, rights.

By August, the UIDAI team was ready for the launch. It dawned on the Congress bigwigs that this was a big moment, an opportunity to communicate with over a billion people across the country. A group led by Jairam Ramesh, the preferred wordsmith of the high command, then the environment minister, descended on the UIDAI office to suggest the wording and wordage. The team resisted, uncomfortable with politicising the programme. Eventually, a consensus was arrived at, enabled by Sharma. The tagline of the party was 'Congress *ka haath, aam aadmi ke saath* (Hand of Congress with the common man)'. A derivation of the slogan was extended to the Aadhaar programme. The identity card would carry, at the bottom of the demographic data, the line 'Aadhaar – *Aam aadmi ka adhikar* (Right of the common man)'.

The optics of the programme and the location were to be decided by the political regime. The Gandhi family

The Know Who Factor

has an association with Nandurbar in Maharashtra. Indira Gandhi had addressed a rally in the district during her campaign in 1967 and, in 1998, Sonia Gandhi, soon after taking over the Congress, held her first rally there. Not surprisingly then, Tembhali in Nandurbar was the chosen venue for the national launch of the Aadhaar card. It isn't just political history that drove that choice, though. Nandurbar has the lowest human development indicator in Maharashtra, is a predominantly tribal area, suffers from poor connectivity and has persistently ranked at the bottom of the per capita income table in the state. The location of the launch was part of Aadhaar's political syntax.

On 29 September 2010, the welcome arches at Tembhali proclaimed, 'Pragatiche mahadwar ugadnar Aadhaar' in Marathi. Roughly translated, Aadhaar will open the doors of progress. Sonia Gandhi, accompanied by Manmohan Singh and Ashok Chavan, launched the Aadhaar card. The first Aadhaar number was issued to home-maker Ranjana Sonawane of Tembhali village. Speaking at the launch, Sonia Gandhi declared, 'Aadhaar will give the poor the right to all government schemes, especially in places like Nandurbar where tribal people still don't benefit from welfare schemes.'

The launch in Tembhali kicked off enrolment across states. The process was not without its riddles. For instance, residents were asked to bring any document that helped the process of identification. This triggered the question, why did the person need to bring a document of identity if UIDAI was to establish and provide identification?

Sharma agrees it is a valid question. 'Document is a circular problem. If I have a document, why do I need a document? But there has to be a process. UIDAI put out a menu of documents – seventeen options for proof of address and nineteen options for proof of identity. If they didn't have a document, we had a system of introduction – from a village Pradhan, MLA, somebody.' Sharma says the overriding principle was 'ensuring inclusion'.

A rumour that went viral around this time proclaimed that there was a dress code for enrolment. In a country where every thread and stitch can acquire political colour, this could have proved to be a speed-breaker. The government had to address the issue across media platforms and clarify that everyone was free to wear any kind and colour of dress at the time of enrolment, 'provided it does not hide any part of the face'. Moreover, there was no bar on wearing a turban, a burkha or any religious–traditional headgear while being photographed.

On 16 November 2010, a fortnight after the formal launch, UIDAI touched 100,000 enrolments when it issued a unique identity number to Lakshmamma from Tumkur, in Karnataka. On 13 January 2011, fifteen-year-old Sukrity, a resident of North Tripura, became the one-millionth resident to enrol for Aadhaar.

4

Push for the Pull

IDENTIFYING IDEAS FOR ACCELERATION

It had taken the UIDAI a good 106 days to touch the one million mark. Impressive as this was by normative government standards, enrolment coverage was quite a distance from the eventual goal. To be precise, it was 1,199,000,000, or one thousand one hundred and ninety-nine million away from 1.2 billion Aadhaar numbers.

For perspective, compare this with another set of numbers. One thousand one hundred and ninety-nine million is the combined population of the US and all the twenty-eight countries in the European Union plus Brazil and Russia. Nilekani, Nadhamuni and Koshy had recognised and recorded the need to create a push for the pull factor in the early conversations and they had factored it even as they planned the setting up of UIDAI. Whether there was enough of a pull factor in their ideas to generate those one billion enrolments would now be truly tested.

Flashback to 28 June 2009. Two days after the announcement of the unique identity project, Shankar Maruwada called Nilekani to congratulate him on his new assignment. Maruwada, ace at humanising marketing analytics, is an IIT Kharagpur graduate who went on to IIM Ahmedabad before taking up brand management at Proctor & Gamble. Infected by the entrepreneurial bug, he got on board the internet boom in 2000 and in 2003, started Marketics, and continued to head it even after it was bought over by WNS Holdings, a global business process outsourcing giant. In the summer of 2009, he decided to call it quits. After which, he says, 'I had more time than I knew what to do with.' Maruwada had started working with Nilekani well before he officially joined in December with the title Head of Demand Generation and Marketing.

By design, governments are supply-driven. Decisions on investment, expenditure and welfare programmes are propelled by forecasts, estimates enabled by demographics and assumptions – even if it does not always pan out as predicted. Frequently, these are extrapolations – a la the poultry farm arithmetic of X number of hens equals Y number of eggs equals an output of Z. Also, programmes are crafted on the basis of existing or perceived wants and needs. What governments tend to not do is dwell as much is on generation of demand. And there is good reason for this. For one, government programmes are typically behind the curve on wants and needs and are catching up. More pertinently, they are backed by executive orders or by statutory provisions, so there is no need for the system to convince people to queue up.

For example, those who want to drive motor vehicles must apply for a driver's licence. Families wanting subsidised food grains must have a ration card. Individuals filing income tax returns must apply for a PAN card number. Voters need their photo identity card and investors wishing to play the stock market or park their savings in mutual funds must have an account with a depository. In effect, the want factor is backed by need, the need to possess. The team at UIDAI was keenly aware that Aadhaar enrolment was not mandated as compulsory. Ergo, there was no explicit compulsion to get in the queue for enrolment.

To create a need to possess, and then drive this need, Maruwada put in place an advisory committee. In February 2010, an Awareness and Communication Strategy Advisory Council was set up with the founder of Chlorophyll, Kiran Khalap, as chairperson. Members included D.K. Bose of the Centre for Advocacy Research, Praveen Tripathi of Pidilite Industries, Santosh Desai of Future Brands, Sumeet Vohra of P&G, A.K. Pandey and Sumnesh Joshi of UIDAI, and Maruwada. The group met with a diverse set of people, including admen Prasoon Joshi and Prasoon Pandey and scriptwriter Jaideep Sahni – to tap into their understanding of emerging India and its psyche. The Strategy Advisory Council had to recommend communication strategies and additional research studies 'to understand mindsets, attitudes, needs, behaviours, habits, for the diverse target audience'.[1]

The target audience was not at all monolithic. There was India I, which was largely urban, about 100 million in population, which would ask why they should queue up for one more identity card. There was India II, small-town India, which was combative and aspirational, small-town India, the kind that is producing new startupreneurs, comprising around 400 million. India III was largely dependent on the government to survive.

From India III came an insightful lesson – that there may be no demand for a unique identity but there is truckloads of demand for economic assets. The thinking in rural India is not why but why not. As one Nalanda villager told Naman Pugalia, *'Agar sarkar ek aur bhains de to mana karen kya?'* (If the government wants to give us another buffalo, why say no?) The larger point being not about the extra buffalo but about the tools to access entitlement; even if the Aadhaar exercise does not deliver, what is the harm in participating? Since murmurs about privacy had begun around then, Pugalia asked another set of villagers if they were concerned about 'durupayog' (misuse). The response, *'Burbak ho kya? Chhipaaney ke liye kuchh hai hi nahin to kyon daren?'* (Crazy or what? We have nothing to hide, so what should we fear?)

And so the council had to strategise several approaches on various tactical fronts to understand the many markets that constitute India. No communication

Push for the Pull

could be designed down the Madison Avenue route; slick is not trusted. No matter how tacky, government communication is trusted; the four-faced lion, or Sher Chhaap, is still the most trusted symbol. This was validated repeatedly by the volunteer teams focus groups, the Baker Street Irregulars as Nilekani fondly referred to them. Everything these volunteers gleaned was logged in for future reference across functions in the UIDAI. Nilekani would make it a point to sit with them after their field trips to hear, first-hand, their experiences and observations, and the views and reactions that they harvested from across the country. These debriefing sessions also gave all the participants an understanding of the codes of India's social operating systems.

Such learnings influenced the design of the communication strategy: the central theme had to be focussed on benefits and the message had to be kept simple. Context is critical in India. Politicians know this well, which is why campaign words and even tunes are set to geographical and cultural context. Policy, however, is crafted for universal outcomes, which is good, but the politics of policy, acceptance or resistance, are contextual. Team UIDAI tailored its communication for different target groups: state governments, bureaucrats, civil society, institutional partners, local government bodies and corporates. To drive home the message, the Council created a tool box of case studies which dealt with the landscape of policy and the need for identity documents to engender outcomes. One such true story, titled Ram's Wheel, was about Nathu Ram, a villager from Madhya Pradesh.

It was a narration of the hardships Ram went through to collect his MGNREGS dues. He had to walk 6 km to the nearest bus stop. There he had to wait for a bus, which wasn't regular, would arrive over-crowded and might also break down on the way. Then he had to have the money to buy a ticket to find a toehold on that bus and travel 14 km to the nearest bank branch. He then had to wait nearly two hours, in the hope that his turn would come before the bank closed for the day. If he was lucky, he would get his money the same day. If not, he would have to camp on the road outside, until the branch opened on the next working day. Having finally got his dues for the month, Ram would travel back home, 14 km by bus and 6 km by foot. Given the uncertainty of getting his dues from the bank, Ram would have already borrowed from the local money lender at usurious rates. Only after he had repaid that bridge-loan, or a part of it, if he had any money left, would he be able to get to the local fair-price ration shop to buy his family's grains and cooking fuel.

Team UIDAI created a graphic representation of the physical hardships and the monetary loss in terms of wage earning hours lost. If what he went through was added up, Ram lost almost 20 per cent of the amount that the government was giving him. This story and the graphics caught the imagination of the politicos and the babus.

Push for the Pull

The Ram Case Study was a fixture of most presentations and was liked and quoted by the political establishment, from Pranab Mukherjee to Rahul Gandhi.

•

Good communication is vital but not enough to hyper-propel enrolment for a number on a card that not everyone thinks they want or need. Physics tells us that momentum is mass multiplied by velocity. This holds just as true in the political economy, where velocity is determined by the extent of necessary and sufficient conditions. The critical catalyst required for acceleration was utility, and the seeding of the idea of unique identity and Aadhaar into the heart of the discourse on public expenditure and delivery of public services. To this end, the objective was to create branding and brand recall in the public domain and in conversations. This was crafted through the corridors of policy at every level of government and at multiple forums: from mentions in the annual budget to the economic survey, in elaboration of the premise of Aadhaar and its promise through documentations that outlined benefits, within departments and at inter-ministerial committees.

The promise of unique identity was first outlined in the Economic Survey of 2009–10. 'The UID System is envisioned as a means for residents to easily establish their identity, anywhere in the country. It will be an important step towards ensuring that residents in India can access the resources and benefits they are entitled to.'[2]

It was underlined in the president's address to Parliament. Pratibha Patil, then the president, said, 'To reach the millions of underprivileged people, my Government has launched a unique Aadhaar scheme which would help improve service delivery, accountability and transparency in social sector programmes and lead to their financial inclusion.'[3]

The 13th Finance Commission, chaired by Vijay Kelkar, said, 'We propose to incentivise issue of UIDs to those people below the poverty line who are beneficiaries of public welfare schemes.' The Commission decided to pay Rs 100 per person and created a grant of Rs 29.89 billion for state governments.[4]

Prime Minister Manmohan Singh too projected its potential. At the 55th National Development Council Meeting, he presented the unique identity programme as an instrument to reduce fiscal deficit and deliver succour to the poor. 'The operationalization of the Unique Identification Number Scheme, together with developments in information technology, provides an opportunity to target subsidies effectively to those who really need them and deserve them.'[5] At an interaction with newspaper editors, he said, 'We need system reforms. If the UIDAI can give unique ID numbers to all our residents we would have discovered a new pathway to eliminate the scope for corruption and leakages in distribution of subsidies.'[6]

Finance Minister Pranab Mukherjee, chief evangelist of the idea 'close to his heart', ensured that he not only

Push for the Pull

mentioned it in every budget speech but wherever he spoke about effective governance, whether within the party, at conferences of chief ministers, cabinet meetings or in Parliament. Making a *suo motu* statement on inflation in November 2011, he presented Aadhaar as an instrument to protect the poor from the vagaries of market forces. He said, 'Government is working to improve delivery of benefits including subsidies to the vulnerable sections of the population using the UIDAI platform'.[7]

Meanwhile, Nilekani and his core team were readying a library of solutions – internally referred to as sleeper cells – for as and when, and if, a problem arose. Governments live with problems like they are fixtures, only taking note when it morphs into a full-fledged crisis. When this happens, government looks for documentation of the problem and solutions. This is because no problem is really new or has not been discussed in the system. And documentation creates an opening, like in a chess game, for the next move. Team UIDAI had played their own devil's advocate, anticipated and forecast some issues, and brainstormed the solutions – all of this even before the first code for software for the enrolment process had been written. They had also chronicled what more they could do, and how they would do it. The first Strategy Overview, for instance, discusses the use of Aadhaar for opening accounts, for doorstep banking via micro-ATMs. It said, 'Linking the UID number to a universal, accessible, and affordable micropayments model can transform the access the poor have to banking services.'

The way forward was to map the landscape of services that needed proof of identity and proof of address and embed Aadhaar as the solution. This leverage was embedded in its 28 January 2009 notification which specifically enabled UIDAI to 'define usage and applicability of UID for delivery of various services'. It also said that UIDAI should 'define mechanisms and processes for interlinking UID with partner databases on a continuous basis'.[8]

To catalyse this process, team UIDAI created a bank of Aadhaar-enabled solutions and put it out in the public domain. This included 'Envisioning a Role for Aadhaar in the Public Distribution System', 'Discussion Paper on Aadhaar-based Financial Inclusion', 'UID and Education', 'UID and NREGA', 'UID and Public Health' and 'Leveraging Aadhaar in the Telecom Sector'. Flanking, or building around the central idea of identification with reports, was aimed at promoting early adoption, expansion and immortality.

The first stop of this strategy was banking. Throughout UPA I and II, the Manmohan Singh government was very keen on improving financial inclusion. Nearly two-thirds of Indians did not have bank accounts, or as the government and bankers say, were 'unbanked'. The problem had two facets: access to banking and access to banks. Access to banking was haunted by poor processes – a primary cause being lack of documents for identification. Access to banks was essentially hampered by the fact there were not enough bank branches. India had a total of 83,997 branches. Rural India with over 600,000 villages was served by just 32,289 branches.[9]

Team UIDAI's approach was two-pronged. First, get Aadhaar approved as a valid KYC document by banks, so those who had access to banks could open accounts. Second, present hand-held micro ATMs and other Aadhaar-enabled processes as solutions that would enable the creation of an ecosystem for banking to be possible. Towards this, UIDAI continuously looked at opportunities to be part of any problem-solving platforms or committees and embedded itself in government committees on financial inclusion.

On 11 December 2009, the Reserve Bank of India held a meeting with the Indian Banks Association, the Institute for Development and Research on Banking Technology, India Post, NABARD and a number of banks on Aadhaar-based financial inclusion. Two working groups were formed to address technology and connectivity issues. UIDAI mobilised opinion for the adoption of Aadhaar as KYC with the banks. There was initial resistance from RBI. The Ministry of Finance pushed for acceptance, and by December 2010, a few weeks after the Tembhali launch, Aadhaar was cleared as valid KYC for opening bank accounts.

There was an element of serendipity too – a series of events coalesced to deliver the perfect conditions for quantum change. The need for modernising payment systems in banks was first highlighted in a 2001 Vision Document of RBI. In 2005, the RBI revisited the idea and put out Vision Document II after studying payment systems in the US, UK, Europe, Japan, Singapore and China.[10] Its stated mission was 'the establishment of safe, secure, sound and efficient payment and settlement systems for the country'. In 2008, post legislation and guidelines,[11] an entity to do this was finally cleared.

In December that year, the government created the National Payments Corporation of India (NPCI), with ten big banks as promoters, to integrate retail payment systems and create the infrastructure for an affordable payment mechanism. The UIDAI team seized the opportunity and began discussions with RBI, NPCI and the banks. NPCI was the perfect platform to set up applications for expanding inclusion through electronic transfer of funds, scholarships, subsidies, micro ATMs and so on.

The second serendipitous event was the massive expansion of mobile phone subscription across India. In 2010, India's population was 1,210 million. Of these, less than a fourth had a bank account. Although the official score was over 600 million accounts, unique individual bank accounts were estimated to be around 250 million. On 31 July 2010, fifteen years after the first cellular mobile phone call was made by Telecom Minister Sukh Ram in Delhi to West Bengal Chief Minister Jyoti Basu, India had 635.5 million mobile phone subscribers.

The scale of mobile telephony penetration provided

a huge opportunity for NPCI to create payment systems and for UIDAI to plan applications. Technology and innovative policies could combine to give Indians the options to bank whenever, wherever, however with the help of devices and applications. In November 2009, the government set up an Inter-Ministerial Group on Provision of Basic Financial Services through Mobile Phones with a subgroup of NPCI, UIDAI and the Department of Technology. In April 2010, the government approved a framework for providing financial services through mobile phones – through a mobile-based PIN system using 'Mobile Banking POS' and through a fingerprint-based system using Aadhaar numbers.

Migration from problem to solution is rarely a linear path, in the government and even in the private sector. It calls for orchestration of thoughts and organisation of action. In an early interaction over a Chinese lunch, Mukherjee and Nilekani had a long conversation about inducting technology for governance. In the Budget of 2010–11, Mukherjee created the high-level Technology Advisory Group for Unique Projects (TAGUP) with Nilekani as its chairman.

TAGUP was mandated to advise the government on developing systems 'for an effective tax administration and financial governance system through creation of IT projects which are reliable, secure and efficient'. The projects included the Tax Information Network, the New Pension Scheme, the New Treasury Management Agency, the Expenditure Information Network and the

Goods and Services Tax. TAGUP recommended the creation of National Information Utilities in a unique private–public partnership where companies would be private so as to be able to attract talent and for speed but with the government retaining strategic control.[12]

Mukherjee and Manmohan Singh also drafted Nilekani into many committees, including the Committee on Electronic Toll Collection, the National Advisory Group on e-Governance, the Expert Committee on HR Policy for e-Governance, the Review Committee on JNNURM, the Reserve Bank of India Advisory Group on Corporate Governance, the IT Task Force for Power Sector and the National Council on Skill Development. At one point, activists from civil society groups, members of the NAC and others raised the issue that Nilekani was a member of committees that deeply influenced the penetration of Aadhaar.

The government was primarily focussed on leakages and its impact on the gap between its income and expenditure, also known as fiscal deficit. A series of reports sequenced the way forward for government to manage the ballooning Subsidy Bill. The Task Force on IT Strategy for PDS recommended an institutional mechanism to implement end-to-end computerisation. It suggested the constitution of a National Information Utility called the Public Distribution System Network to implement and operate the IT infrastructure for PDS.

The Task Force on Reforms in Subsidy Distribution System recommended the creation of a core subsidy management system for transparency in movement of goods, levels of stocks, demand and identification of beneficiaries. This was followed by a Task Force on Direct Transfer of Subsidies on Kerosene, LPG and Fertilisers to Individual Families. In its report released in June 2011, the Task Force proposed a general framework for transfer of subsidies and a phased move to direct transfer of benefits, where the subsidy would be transferred to the beneficiary's account.[13]

This idea was expanded upon by the Task Force on Aadhaar Enabled Unified Payment Infrastructure. It recommended that payment of subsidies, pensions and scholarships should be electronically transferred into accounts of the beneficiary's choice, whether at banks or post offices. The Task Force also recommended that the wages of teachers, aanganwadi workers and health care volunteers be directly transferred. Given the limited penetration of banks, the government brought in another committee to set standards for micro ATMs. It recommended that business correspondents of banks be equipped with micro ATMs that could create a network for doorstep banking.

Action followed thought. Finance Minister Mukherjee urged bankers to push financial inclusion and underline the importance of Aadhaar enrolments and Aadhaar-enabled bank accounts to deliver services and entitlements to the marginalised sections of society.[14] Prime Minister Manmohan Singh pushed for setting up systems for the direct transfer of MGNREGS wages and of pensions, scholarships and LPG subsidies to bank accounts. Ministries were asked to create a digital list of beneficiaries. Focusing on subsidies, Mukherjee, Agriculture Minister Sharad Pawar and Food Minister K.V. Thomas addressed a meeting of state food ministers and underlined the need for reforms in PDS, issue of biometric cards, identification of beneficiaries for various categories, elimination of bogus ration cards and improvement in the Targeted Public Distribution System besides persistent issues of procurement and storage.

The Planning Commission and UIDAI were tasked with consulting and interacting with the departments of food and civil supplies and agriculture as well as state governments to map the way ahead.

•

ARTICLE 1(1) of the Constitution of India says, 'India, that is Bharat, shall be a Union of States'. Engrained in that one sentence, and defined by the distribution of powers in Part XI, is the federal structure of governance. This calls for collaboration and cooperation between the Centre and the states.

The political reality of India is that virtually every square mile is ruled by the states. The Centre, former Andhra Chief Minister N.T. Rama Rao once said, was a conceptual myth. Perhaps this characterisation is an exaggeration, but the fact is that the issues that UIDAI sought to address mostly fell in the remit of the states. The public distribution system, fertiliser subsidies and

Push for the Pull

kerosene subsidies were administered by the states. States also were in charge of ensuring last-mile delivery of pensions, wages under the national rural employment programme and scholarships to needy students.

It was, therefore, important to engage with, and be able to persuade, the states to push the idea of Aadhaar. The hub-and-spoke architecture of Aadhaar enrolment required UIDAI to collaborate with the states. The states wanted clarity on the two initiatives: NPR enrolment and Aadhaar enrolment. It turned out that states which had their own identity cards asked, 'Why another?'

Rajasthan, for instance, had the Bhamashah card. It was named after Bhamashah, a warrior and confidante of the legendary Maharana Pratap. The scheme was introduced in February 2008 by the Vasundhara Raje-led BJP government.[15] Under Bhamashah, the state government opened an account with Rs 1,500 in it in the name of the woman of the house for families from marginalised sections of society. The state had identified about five million women. In the run-up to the 2008 polls, activists had approached the High Court and got a stay on the scheme.[16] After the Congress government of Ashok Gehlot came to power in November 2008, the officials in the Rajasthan government wanted to hitch the Bhamashah scheme to the Aadhaar bandwagon. Eventually, the Gehlot regime, convinced about the universal nature of the UIDAI project, adopted Aadhaar.

Many states sought to adapt before they adopted Aadhaar. The Aadhaar template allowed for just four fields – name, age, gender and communication address. Some states wanted the data field to be expanded. Their explanation was that the data would help improve their quality of services and target welfare better.

Within the UIDAI, Nilekani and Sharma were divided over the issue. The technology team intervened and said it would slow down the process, since the additional queries would make the enrolment process longer. The legal team pointed out that additional questions went beyond the mandate of UIDAI. Sharma argued for a way to accommodate all positions and in the end, the states were allowed to collect the additional data; this created momentum to get them on board.

The compromise was that a program would be written – the code for it would be organised by the states – to allow states to simultaneously record the data in a separate file. Managing the files and finding storage was the states' responsibility. The expanded version was christened KYR Plus or Know Your Resident Plus. Andhra Pradesh was among the first states to seek this change. Other states too found the plus format alluring. The enrolling agencies collected these new fields which related to ration and BPL card details, size of family, ownership of assets, PAN card, etc.

UIDAI had made it clear that this data would not be part of the Aadhaar records or hosted on their servers. This created a complication. The states didn't have space to digitally store the data. This was resolved by a Sharma-led innovation: a state resident data hub,

Push for the Pull

akin to digital locker services. The management and responsibility for the storage hub rested with the states.

On the ground, the collection of additional data and answers for new queries did slow down the process of enrolment. More importantly, many people who came to enrol went back without doing so. The documentation required for the additional queries was daunting. The states also found that the data they collected wasn't serving any real purpose and was leading to exclusion. Many states gave up along the way.

One of the states that successfully designed and organised KYR Plus was Gujarat. Initially, the Gujarat government was sceptical of the UIDAI idea. Also, the state was already trying methods to link the public distribution system with biometric data. Nilekani had met the officials of the Gujarat government on 8 December 2009, and a State Cabinet Council on Unique Identification Project was in place by March 2010. But progress was slow.

Nilekani met Narendra Modi, then chief minister of Gujarat, again on 26 July 2011. The meeting lasted well over an hour.[17] Chief Minister Modi raised several questions and suggested that the technology team visit Gujarat. He wanted the technology features to be leveraged to enhance national security and to utilise human resources to optimum capacity in different areas. Nilekani agreed to arrange a workshop for the Gujarat government team.

The meeting found mention on narendramodi.in as

follows: 'Today's meet is likely to open up new avenues in public service, particularly the multiple utility aspects of the Unique ID project in a much broader sense.' Thereafter the Gujarat government convened the Council on 4 August 2011 to design a unique KYR Plus with special features. Additional demographics included Electoral Photo Identity Card number, Ration Card number, BPL Card number and RSBY Card number, details of disability and LPG/PNG gas connection and proof of unique household number for urban slums.[18] This was then formalised through a Government Resolution.[19]

On 1 May 2012, Chief Minister Modi joined many others, to give his biometric and demographic data for an Aadhaar number.[20] Soon enough, the pace picked up. The ramping up of enrolment by Gujarat had a demonstration effect on other states, especially the BJP-ruled states. By October 2012, two years after the launch of Aadhaar at Tembhali, 210 million unique identity numbers had been issued.

5

Law and Political Order

WHO IS UIDAI, ASKS THE OPPOSITION

When Nilekani met with Manmohan Singh back in June 2009 to discuss his entry into the government, he had six must-get issues on his list. One of them was a law to statutorily back the UIDAI. The prime minister assured him that a law bestowing statutory authority to the autonomous body would be prioritised. By the summer of 2010, many murmurs and questions about legalities had surfaced. What was UIDAI? Who exactly was UIDAI? Did it have legal sanction?

There were letters to the prime minister, to the chairperson of NAC, Sonia Gandhi, commentary in the media and questions in Parliament. Between June 2009 and June 2010, Members of Parliament, twenty-three from the Lok Sabha and sixteen from the Rajya Sabha, questioned the government about the form, function and funding of the UIDAI programme and, more pertinently, what it meant for the multipurpose national identity card being issued by the Home Ministry.

UIDAI needed legitimacy to roll out a programme that would touch the lives of millions. The worries were valid. Following consultations within government, with stakeholders in civil society and legal pundits, UIDAI prepared the draft for a legislation to provide statutory status and structure, with powers and protections, for Aadhaar enrolments. Meanwhile, the team also thought about expanding their consultation process so all concerns could be addressed. They sought a meeting with the Parliamentary Standing Committee on Finance which was headed by senior BJP leader Yashwant Sinha.

Sinha recalls that he was intrigued by the request for a meeting. The question was, what locus standi did UIDAI have to ask for a meeting and what possible rationale could justify it. The committee, by convention, met to discuss matters before it. How could it meet to discuss a hypothesis? Sinha says, 'We found a way out. The logic was that the project dealt with addressing issues of subsidies and this had consequences on government expenditure. So it was decided that they could do a presentation.'

The MPs grilled Nilekani and the UIDAI team on many issues, including those occupying public mindspace. Nilekani recalls the meeting as 'a great experience'. In a television interview he later said of the meeting, 'Let me tell you, this is a very rigorous process. I have been around the world. I have visited the UK Parliament, the French Parliament and the US House. They know what they are asking. I am very impressed.'[1] He also expressed confidence in the process and said that 'we should respect them for the work that they do'. Nilekani would come to discover that he had discounted the vagaries, the fickle nature of politics.

On 29 June 2010, UIDAI put out a draft of the legislation, the National Identification Authority of India Bill 2010.[2] The justification stated that the UIDAI was functioning under an executive order and there was a need to establish a statutory authority for the purpose of carrying out the mandate of issuing unique identification numbers to the residents of India. The draft Bill proposed the landscape of the authority's powers and functions. The note was also circulated to all the ministries for their comments.

The Ministry of Home Affairs was the first to respond with comments.[3] They found four problems with the Bill, including its name. The Home Ministry wanted the name to be changed as it clashed with the acronym for the National Investigation Agency under MHA. It objected to the provisions that allowed audit of the data with the NPR. It also questioned the legalities of the MoU that would have to be signed between the department under MHA and the UIDAI. And they wanted the norms of disclosure of information under national security to be spelt out in the Act or in the Rules. Other ministries followed with their issues.

Meanwhile civil society groups and activists were questioning the very need for UIDAI to exist. Activist and commentator Praful Bidwai said, 'There is no clarity about the project's purpose and the legitimacy of one of its principal functions.'[4] He added that 'all manner of claims are made about its virtues and potential to contribute to governance'. Reetika Khera, development economist at the Delhi School of Economics, wrote that 'tall claims' were being made. 'Nilekani speaks of how having "UID can give automatic benefits".[5] In practice, there will be automatic exclusion as those who do not enrol will be turned away.' She added that lessons must be learnt from how linking NREGA accounts with bank accounts resulted in 'no account, no work'.[6]

On 20 August 2010, the birth anniversary of Prime Minister Rajiv Gandhi, the Rural Development Ministry announced a project to roll out the nationwide biometric database of NREGA workers in collaboration with UIDAI at a workshop titled 'Mahatma Gandhi NREGA Making ICT an Instrument for People's Entitlement: A step towards governance reform and transparency' in Vigyan Bhawan, Delhi. In attendance at what was billed as a signal political event were C.P. Joshi, Jairam Ramesh, Montek Singh Ahluwalia, Sam Pitroda and Nilekani.

There was fiery backlash from activists. Members of the National Advisory Council sent a letter to Rural Development Minister C.P. Joshi. Jean Dreze and Aruna Roy pointed out that the project did not have the clearance of the Central Employment Guarantee Council.[7] They said, 'It would be particularly dangerous and inappropriate to proceed with any linking before the legislative framework of the UID project has been worked out. We suggest that decisions related to the linking of UID with NREGA are put on hold in the meantime.'

For Dreze it was about the linkage to welfare programmes but more fundamentally it was about liberty. 'I am opposed to the UID project on grounds of civil liberties. Let us not be naive. This is not a social policy initiative – it is a national security project.'[8] The Orwellian state was a recurring theme at discussions then, just as Big Brother has been in 2016 and 2017.

The issue of privacy had come up earlier too, in December 2009. Neeraj Shekhar, Samajwadi Party MP from Uttar Pradesh, had raised the issue of privacy and rights of a citizen. He had asked whether the confidentiality of personal details of individuals would be at risk after the issue of unique identities. He had enquired whether the government needed to bring a privacy policy to safeguard the same and how the project would maintain a balance between the privacy of individuals and the requirement of security agencies.[9] Minister of Planning V. Narayansamy, in his reply clarified that 'the Unique Identification Authority of India (UIDAI) will not share resident data unless required by law. A legal framework is being envisaged to safeguard the privacy of the resident's data and also take care of the security requirements of the country.'

•

The UIDAI core team had examined the issue of privacy in its earliest days, in the E-403 Bengaluru tower office. Nadhamuni, Koshy, Mashruwala, Varma and others had discussed it at great length, and in November 2009, Nilekani and the team had spoken of it with officials at MHA. Accordingly, they articulated in their Strategy Overview, 'The UIDAI envisions a balance between "privacy and purpose" when it comes to the information it collects.' It also envisaged that 'necessary provisions would be in place to address the issues of privacy and confidentiality'.

The question was how to ensure such a balance. UIDAI consulted Rahul Matthan, an expert on privacy laws and a founding partner at Trilegal, and others, including Kamlesh Bajaj, CEO of the Data Security Council of India. They also talked to telecom and cable companies, industry bodies and other experts. Ram Sewak Sharma engaged with officials in government formally and informally. The government, particularly the top bureaucrats in the system, was also concerned about the emerging challenges of managing the collected data and its uses.

A committee of secretaries under the chairmanship of Cabinet Secretary K.M. Chandrashekhar was formed to study and recommend a 'Legal framework for data protection and security and privacy norms' for the UIDAI. It included Sudha Pillai, secretary, Planning Commission; Home Secretary G.K. Pillai; IT Secretary R. Chandrashekhar; DIPP Secretary R.P. Singh;

Revenue Secretary Sunil Mitra; Dr T. Ramasami, secretary, Science and Technology; Dr D.R. Meena, secretary, Legal Affairs; R. Gopalan, secretary, Financial Services; Shantanu Consul, secretary, Personnel; R. Chandramouli, the registrar general of India and Ram Sewak Sharma of UIDAI. In the loop were T.K.A. Nair, principal secretary to prime minister and National Security Adviser Shiv Shankar Menon.

The briefing note for the 20 May 2010 meeting stated upfront that 'The security and protection of personal data being collected by various government and private agencies is in question because of a gap in the law as there is no data protection legislation in India. India will need to start thinking about these issues in a comprehensive and systematic manner.'[10]

The committee of secretaries looked at global practices. It examined several aspects. What should be the scope of the law? How should personal data be defined? How can the legal framework enable transparency in the collection and use of data, what should be the standard framework for security of data and what kind of an oversight mechanism should be created? They focussed on collection, processing, disclosure, access and accountability for disclosure of data besides standards for government and private agencies, definition of security, and definitions of civil and criminal liabilities.

On 5 July 2010, the Data Security Council of India put out a consultation paper titled 'Legal Framework for Data Protection and Security and Privacy Norms' and submitted it to the Department of Personnel and Training in the Government of India. This led to the hosting of a Workshop on Legal Framework for Privacy, Data Protection and Security at the Civil Services Officers Institute in Delhi on 21 July 2010.[11]

Among the twenty-two experts present were sixteen officers from the government, from the Department of Personnel and Training (DoPT), the ministries of Home Affairs, IT, Finance, Telecom and Law, NatGrid CEO Raghu Raman, and experts from the private sector, including Matthan of Trilegal; Bajaj from DSCI; Sunil Abraham, executive director, Centre for Internet & Society; M.R. Umarji, chief legal adviser to the Indian Banks Association; Arunima Sharma, deputy director of CII; director of the Centre for Internet Society, Anuradha Das Mathur; founder director 9.9 Media and others. Shantanu Consul, secretary, DoPT, kicked off the deliberations by highlighting the need for a comprehensive privacy law for India and also detailed the formation of a group to lay down a legal framework.

The workshop explored the contours of the legal landscape. Among the questions raised were: is privacy a fundamental right? Does a citizen voluntarily give his personal information to government databases or is there a threat of services being denied to them? C. Chandramouli, registrar general of India, pointed the participants to a significant fact: census data is confidential as per the Census Act 1948. This data is not to be disclosed even to the courts of law. He also revealed that every request for disclosure made under RTI had been rejected under Section 8(1)(j) of the RTI Act. Gulshan Rai, DG, Department of IT, presented the provisions for data protection under the IT Act 2000. M.R. Umarji pointed out that legal protection was embedded in the existing laws on banking – obligation of secrecy is implied in the contract between banker and customer. So, in a sense, the issue of privacy had been a consideration in Indian laws, even if segmented in silos.

The consensus opinion, articulated by Rajeev Kapoor, joint secretary AT&A, DoPT, was that while there were provisions in existing laws, there was a 'need for an umbrella legislation on the subject which should enable sector specific guidelines to be framed'. He mentioned that the framework would have to strike the right balance between the 'Right to Information' and the 'Right to Privacy'.

Besides and beyond Aadhaar, the context of emerging technologies, the expansion of e-governance and the arrival of mobile communications and e-commerce created a sense of urgency. A core group got together and authored a draft legislation which was presented to the committee of secretaries headed by the cabinet secretary and was also put out in the public domain in October 2010 for consultations.[12]

•

Towards the end of 2010, it was agitprop politics that steered the course of events.

On 4 September 2010, the Union Cabinet cleared the National Identification Authority of India 2010 Bill. That evening, the government announced that the Bill proposed to constitute a statutory authority to be called the National Identification Authority of India and lay down the powers and functions of the Authority, the framework for issuing UID/Aadhaar numbers, major penalties and other related matters through an Act of Parliament. The Bill was to be introduced in the winter session of Parliament in December.

The bill's clearance by the cabinet stirred a hornet's nest. A group of academics, jurists, activists and film-makers launched a 'Campaign for No UID'.[13] Besides the fear of privacy violations, the group declared that there had been scarce and limited discussion on the consequences and implications of the project. Their core demand was that the project be halted and a feasibility study undertaken. The signatories included Justice V.R. Krishna Iyer, historians Romila Thapar and Uma Chakravarti, senior civil liberties lawyer K.G. Kannabiran, Kavita Srivastava of PUCL and the Right to Food Campaign, Aruna Roy and Nikhil Dey of Mazdoor Kisan Shakti Sangathan, Gopal Krishna of Citizens Forum for Civil Liberties, Prakash Ray of JNU Researchers Association, Upendra Baxi, former vice-chancellor of Delhi University, and film-makers Shohini Ghosh and Amar Kanwar.

Some of those who protested had been close to the party or to Sonia Gandhi before the Congress-led

UPA came to power in 2004. After she took charge of the Congress in 1998, Sonia Gandhi had multiple interactions with Communist ideologue Mohit Sen, who had known the Nehru–Gandhi family, to understand where to position the Congress. As part of the exercise she met with many activists and groups. Among them were Aruna Roy and Nikhil Dey, who were campaigning for a law for Freedom of Information. The Congress did not want to lose the goodwill of these groups; back-channel conversations were set up with them.

The Manmohan Singh regime went ahead with its legislative agenda. On 3 November, the government announced the schedule of business for the winter session of Parliament slated to start on 9 November. The Congress-led UPA planned to push fifty-eight legislations in twenty-four sittings – the legislative agenda included twenty-three new bills. The National Identification Authority of India 2010 was Bill No. 20 on the list. The government was already facing a barrage of questions on the legitimacy of the UIDAI's operations. Brinda Karat, CPM MP from the Rajya Sabha, asked the government 'under what provisions of law was the UIDAI created'.[14]

On 3 December 2010, Planning Minister V. Narayansamy introduced the National Identification Authority of India Bill 2010 in the Rajya Sabha. The Bill was introduced amidst high-decibel rhetoric. The house was disrupted repeatedly as the BJP-led Opposition cornered the Congress. Any hope of getting the legislation passed appeared dim. Post introduction, the Bill was sent to the Parliamentary Standing Committee on Finance.

The committee first took briefings and oral evidence from the Ministry of Planning and UIDAI. On 29 June 2011, it heard the views of stakeholders, civil society groups and institutional representatives. These included the Human Rights Commission, the Indian Banks Association, independent law researcher Dr Usha Ramanathan, Dr Reetika Khera from the Delhi School of Economics, Associate Professor at TISS Dr R. Ramkumar, and Gopal Krishna of Citizens Forum for Civil Liberties.

The issues that were flagged ranged from legitimacy to biometrics and privacy to whether the programme was needed at all. Those who appeared before the committee questioned the capacity of the state, the state of infrastructure, and suggested that the project would result in exclusion, not inclusion. The activists alerted the committee that the government of Britain had abandoned its ID project, namely the Identity Cards Act 2006. The London School of Economics expressed the view that though the project had the potential to create significant benefits, it was 'too complex, technically unsafe, overly prescriptive and lacked a foundation of public trust and confidence'. The activists quoted the LSE report, and cited a range of reasons including cost, reliability and the changing relationship between the state and the citizen, to argue against the project.

The committee examined the contours of the project

and questioned why a scheme originally intended (in 2006) for BPL families was extended to all residents and other categories of individuals. The Ministry of Planning explained, 'The UID scheme was extended to all residents and other categories' of individuals to gradually do away with the de novo exercises each time for field level data collection. Simultaneously, it would ensure that links to more and more identity based databases were created by inclusion of the UID number in their databases.'

The hearings threw up an interesting debate on the limits of executive power and sovereignty of Parliament. In a written representation to the chairman of the standing committee, Justice Dr M. Rama Jois, MP (Rajya Sabha), pointed out that since the Bill was pending consideration, the issuing of Aadhaar numbers and incurring expenditure from the exchequer was a circumvention of Parliament and should, therefore, be kept in abeyance.

On the issue of UIDAI's legitimacy, the government responded with the opinion of the attorney general of India. Obtained by the Ministry of Law and Justice, it stated: 'The competence of the Executive is not limited to take steps to implement the law proposed to be passed by Parliament. Executive Power operates independently. The Executive is not implementing the provisions of the Bill. The Authority presently functioning under the Executive Notification dated 28th January, 2009 is doing so under valid authority and there is nothing in law or otherwise which prevents the Authority from functioning under the Executive Authorisation.'[15]

While the committee conducted its hearings, a spate of articles and opinions appeared online and in news publications, questioning the basis of Aadhaar, of it not being voluntary and about privacy. Usha Ramanathan argued that 'the myth of voluntariness stands exploded even as it is stated' and pointed out that 'the compulsion will not come from the UIDAI, but other agencies may demand that a person must have a UID number to be provided a service'.[16] Supreme Court advocate Pavan Duggal wrote, 'Unique Identification numbers or Aadhaar numbers are being touted as the next big thing. The current implementation of the UID numbers framework in India is, however, likely to lead to a direct contravention of citizens' fundamental right of privacy.'[17]

There were some delicious ironies too. The CPI-ML quoted British Conservative Party politician Theresa May, then the home secretary, saying, 'The national identity card scheme represents the worst of government. It is intrusive and bullying, ineffective and expensive. It is an assault on individual liberty which does not promise a greater good.' Politicians and activists alike were asking, 'What's the "Aadhaar" of the UID Scheme?'[18]

Meanwhile, the process of finalising the draft of the Bill for a law on privacy continued. On 27 May 2011, the committee of secretaries examined the draft Bill and sent it for redrafting. In October 2011, the Home Ministry called for a meeting with officers of DoPT, MHA and IT. It was to specifically look at and relocate many primary laws into one law for privacy, and assess how the powers of interception of communication and data for national security purposes would fit in. Clearly, the law on privacy was enmeshed in many systemic and philosophical issues and was a long way away.

On 8 December, the standing committee met to finalise its view on the National Identification Authority of India Bill 2010. It presented its views and report to Parliament on 11 December. The standing committee trashed the Bill. It said, 'The UID scheme has been conceptualised with no clarity leaving many things to be sorted out during the course of its implementation; and is being implemented in a directionless way with a lot of confusion. The scheme which was initially meant for BPL families has been extended for all residents in India and to certain other persons.'[19]

The standing committee pointed out that 'The Empowered Group of Ministers constituted for the purpose of collating the two schemes namely, the UID and National Population Register (NPR), and to look into the methodology and specifying target for effective completion of the UID scheme, failed to take concrete decision on important issues such as (a) identifying the focussed purpose of the resident identity database; (b) methodology of collection of data; (c) removing the overlapping between the UID scheme and NPR; (d) conferring of statutory authority to the UIDAI since its inception; (e) structure and functioning of the UIDAI; (f) entrusting the collection of data and issue of unique identification number and national identification number to a single authority instead of the present UIDAI and its reconciliation with National Registration Authority.'

The committee said that the scheme was riddled with lacunae and that the government's defence on continuing with the UIDAI programme without conferring statutory status – that is, a law to authorise, regulate and govern its workings – was indefensible. 'The need for conferring statutory status to UIDAI was felt by the government way back in November 2008 but was deferred for more than two years for no reason.' In a stringent critique of the rendered legal opinion, the committee said it was 'constrained to point out that in the instant case, since the law making is underway with the bill being pending, any executive action is as unethical and violative of Parliament's prerogatives as promulgation of an ordinance while one of the Houses of Parliament [is] in session'.

The Congress reacted to this public thrashing by blaming the BJP. Yashwant Sinha, who chaired the committee, rejects the suggestion of political motives and points out, 'Standing Committee reports are finalised after a consensus is arrived at – and there is a provision for filing dissent notes.'

The composition of parliamentary committees tends to be numerically tilted towards the ruling regime. Of the thirty-one members, eight were from the BJP. It is true that the BJP members, including Piyush Goyal, S.S. Ahluwalia and Nishikant Dubey, were critical of the bill's structure and rationale and opposed it but, as Sinha recalls, 'it was not just BJP but even Congress members were against the project'. The Congress had eleven MPs in the committee, including veteran members like N. Dharam Singh, Vijay Darda and Bhakta Charan Das. Only three disagreed with the final report and filed dissent notes.[20] Indeed, the UIDAI had sought a second hearing – to clarify any doubts – but the Congress MPs could not deliver. Sinha says, 'To blame the BJP was convenient for Congress but quite laughable. We had good reasons, and these were listed, for rejecting the idea and the bill.'

It wasn't just the Bill that was trashed. It was a scathing indictment of the UPA government, floundering due to the undefined ideological identity of the coalition, and caught in an internal civil war. In just one week, four major initiatives – the proposal for FDI in retail,[21] the move to hike FDI in insurance,[22] banking reforms[23] and the Bill to grant statutory status to UIDAI – were shown the door.[24] A little more than a year into its second term, the UPA had lost its mojo.

And the Congress, in a state of atrophy, was losing its identity.

6

The Politics of Politics

ASCENT OF DISSENT,
DISPUTES AND DIFFERENCES

In its first term of leading the coalition that called itself the United Progressive Alliance, the Congress had positioned itself as a pro-poor, pro-inclusive growth party. Its politics rested on entitlement economics. It ushered in the RTI Act, created a justiciable employment guarantee scheme, passed the Forest Rights Act 2006 to provide legal sanctity to the rights of tribals, pushed the largest farm loan waiver and leveraged rising revenues to ramp up social sector spending. Blend this with three years of 9-plus per cent growth and the Indo–US nuclear deal, and the party bigwigs came to believe that the party had, like the FDR regime in the United States, delivered a new deal. To them the 2009 victory and the improved tally of 206 seemed like universal affirmation.

To paraphrase Shakespeare, the good they did was interred but the evils of UPA I lingered. For political parties in India, allegations of corruption are par for the course. What was striking in UPA II was the rapid pace at which a procession of scandals lined up. The Congress was tarred by the Opposition during the trust vote scandal. By month eighteen of its second term, the Congress-led UPA was caught in the headlights of a series of scams.

First up was the CWG scam with a tag of over Rs 250 billion. India hosted the Commonwealth Games in October 2010. In the run-up to the games, a preliminary enquiry report by corruption watch dog Central Vigilance Commission found corrupt practices in fifteen of the major projects. Even as the Congress – whose own members had warned the government in 2007 and 2008 – attempted to repudiate this, the mega 2G scam broke. The UPA government had chosen not to auction spectrum for new telecom licences. The decision was called out as crony capitalism by the Opposition in the 2009 polls but they couldn't make it stick at that point of time, for the issue lacked traction among voters. The CBI had meanwhile filed a case against unknown persons under the Prevention of Corruption Act.

On 10 November, the Comptroller and Auditor General of India released its audit report. The CAG had estimated that due to the failure to auction the spectrum, the national exchequer stood to lose Rs 1.76 trillion. Within days, on 14 November, A. Raja, the telecom minister, was asked to resign and Kapil Sibal was given additional charge of the ministry. Among the many PILs pending was one charging Manmohan Singh's office with inaction on permission to file charges against the minister. On 16 November, the CAG report was tabled in Parliament and the BJP-led Opposition brought both the houses to a halt, calling for a joint parliamentary probe into the 2G scam.

In Mumbai, the Congress-led government was caught in the whirlpool of the Adarsh housing scam, which revealed that influential politicians and persons, including relatives of the Congress Chief Minister Ashok Chavan, had been allotted flats in a high-rise building in upmarket Colaba in south Mumbai.

Between 2003 and 2009, reserves of over 40 billion tonnes of coal were allocated to the public sector and private companies. Allegations of a scam were first heard in August in the Rajya Sabha about allocations of coal mines in Odisha.

Like in the 1970s – before the draconian Emergency when citizen's rights were suspended – it was civil society groups which raised the issue of corruption in public. In April 2011, social activist Anna Hazare stepped in to lead a campaign against corruption in high places. On 5 April, Hazare began a fast unto death at Jantar Mantar in Delhi. The move had the blessing of Opposition parties and the people at large. The 'uprising', as it was dubbed, caught the imagination of people across the country and led to a movement called 'India Against Corruption'.

The movement threw up different types of politicos. Arvind Kejriwal, government servant turned activist, split

The Politics of Politics

from Hazare to form the Aam Aadmi Party and became chief minister in Delhi, and by 2017 was embroiled in his own set of scam allegations; the no-nonsense police officer Kiran Bedi later joined the BJP and was made Lieutenant Governor in Puducherry; yoga guru Ramdev, who made a statement by staging a hunger strike at the Ramleela Maidan, now also runs a flourishing enterprise and is competing with FMCG giants.

The idea of a corruption-free India – a challenging aspiration to this day – found mass subscription and was fuelled by the multiplier effect of social media. It was in a sense India's first glimpse of internet-enabled politics. The Congress party, rooted in top-down politics and its reputation uprooted by a technology-enabled campaign, had no clue how to deal with an emergent India.

With no bandwidth, the Congress lost the plot and the management of narrative. UPA II, suffering from body blows from activists and the Opposition, was reeling from internal factionalism as well. During the course of an internal examination of the Why What Who When of the 2G scam, a note had been filed for the PMO. The note, issued by the office of Finance Minister Pranab Mukherjee and made public via RTI filings, suggested that the Finance Ministry under P. Chidambaram – who had moved over to the Home Ministry in 2008 post the 26/11 terror attacks – could have stopped the 2G scam by insisting on the auction of spectrum issued to new licensees. Notwithstanding denials, the bait was laid as headlines screamed '2G war in UPA: Finance Ministry note to PMO indicts Chidambaram'[1]

The BJP pounced on the opportunity. Prakash Javadekar, then spokesperson for the party, declared, 'Ultimately, the cat is out of the bag. It was very clear from day one that Chidambaram agreed to A. Raja's formula for 2-G spectrum allocation. If he had stuck to the Finance Ministry officials' position that spectrum should not be allocated in 2008 at 2001 prices the scam would not have taken place.'[2] The BJP was hopeful that the Supreme Court, which was hearing the 2G scam cases, would take note. The party demanded Chidambaram be sacked.

It didn't help that there had been speculation about a change of guard at the top of the UPA since Manmohan Singh underwent a fourteen-hour open heart bypass surgery in 2009.[3] The speculation intensified every time there was an escalation of turf battles and even when there were routine ones, between the Home Ministry and the Finance Ministry. In April 2011, speculation about a tussle over a Home Ministry missive on the powers of the Central Board of Direct Taxes to tap telephone conversations acquired political overtones.[4]

Almost on cue, there followed reports about the office of Finance Minister Mukherjee being bugged. An electronic sweep conducted by CBDT sleuths found adhesive pasted in his office, in the office of the adviser Omita Paul and that of his private secretary.[5] Mukherjee wrote to the prime minister about the incident.[6] The prime minister directed the matter be probed. A week later, the Home Ministry clarified that the office of the finance minister was not bugged and Mukherjee told reporters that 'it is a bogus theory'.[7] The Opposition was not about to let go of the juice and Sushma Swaraj declared it a 'matter of grave concern. It is India's Watergate and needs to be thoroughly investigated.' She asked, 'Is it that the government was spying on its own Finance Minister? Or is it a corporate house?'[8] Nothing was conclusively proved or disproved in the end, but the news reports did amplify the perception that there was a fight within for the top slot.

The dysfunction at the top echelons of government visited the progress of UIDAI. The Department of Expenditure expressed concern about duplication of costs since six agencies were collecting information – NPR, MGNREGS, BPL census, UIDAI, Rashtriya Swasthya Bima Yojana (RSBY) and bank smart cards. The Ministry of Home Affairs had concerns about the use of the introducer system, and about the role of private agencies in enrolment. The National Informatics Centre believed UID data should be handled by a government data centre. The Ministry of Planning had reservations about the functioning of UIDAI and whether the collection of iris images was necessary.

The battle for administrative territory and authority was playing out between the registrar general of India and the UIDAI. Officials at both RGI and UIDAI were traversing uncharted territory. In June 2011, the UIDAI team began discussions about phase III of the programme – enrolments were slated to cross 200 million by the end of 2011. On 30 August 2011, Ahluwalia, deputy chairman of the Planning Commission, wrote to Home Minister Chidambaram with a copy to UIDAI chief Nilekani on issues of funding, duplication of work and roll out of Aadhaar numbers by UIDAI and MNIC by RGI. Attached was a five-page note by Sudha Pillai, member secretary, Planning Commission. Before the matter could flare up, Manmohan Singh, who had been briefed by Ahluwalia, asked that the HM and UIDAI chairman meet.

On 22 October 2011, Ahluwalia spoke with Chidambaram on the side lines of the 56th Meeting of the National Development Council. Following the chat, Ahluwalia asked the UIDAI team to put up a draft note on how it proposed to proceed. Till then UIDAI had been cleared for the first 100 million as a pilot, and subsequently received a second clearance in December 2010 to enrol up to 200 million. Earlier it was thought that data recorded by UIDAI could be used by NPR. In a note titled 'Next Steps in Roll Out of Aadhaar', Ahluwalia wrote: 'RGI has taken the view that they cannot accept data collected by UIDAI or any other source.' For RGI to accept UIDAI data, the rules would need to be changed and that required legal opinion. The other option was for NPR to complete the exercise without capturing biometrics. The short point of the long note was that, unless a way was found for NPR/RGI to accept UIDAI data and vice versa, there would be an overlap of work and expenditure.

The Politics of Politics

Chidambaram wrote back on 8 November 2011, 'The decision to register all citizens and issue identity cards precedes the formation of UIDAI.' He then pointed out that the mandate of the UIDAI was 'to generate and assign UID to residents'. As per MHA, enrolment was to be done by RGI. He also said that UIDAI was first allowed 100 million enrolments, which was raised to 200 million 'subject to post facto ratification by CC-UIDAI'. Further enrolments – biographic and biometric – would be done by RGI and the 'UIDAI is to carry out the de-duplication'. He also clarified that other data could not be accepted by NPR and cited section, clause and sub-clause for this. The house-to-house enumeration process of NPR, he added, was better than the document-based enrolment of UIDAI. Chidambaram ruled out the suggestion that NPR should carry out the exercise without biometrics. He also asked the Planning Commission to clear the funding for identity (smart) cards and for setting up the NPR database.

The issue of privacy was also hanging fire. The Planning Commission on 5 January constituted a Group of Experts under the Chairmanship of A.P. Shah, former chief justice of Delhi High Court, to identify the privacy issues and prepare a paper to facilitate authoring of the Privacy Bill. The group, apart from Ram Sewak Sharma, Gulshan Rai, Kamlesh Bajaj and Usha Ramanathan, included Rajiv Kapoor, joint secretary, DoPT; Som Mittal, president, NASSCOM; Pranesh Prakash of the Centre for Internet & Society; and Nagesh Singh and

R.K. Gupta, advisers, Planning Commission. The Group of Experts was asked to submit its report by March 2012.

On 19 January, as the issues remained unresolved, Chidambaram wrote to the prime minister: 'There is no clarity on who will capture the biometric data, the RGI or the UIDAI. A few months ago I had requested the Planning Commission to bring a paper to the cabinet or the appropriate cabinet committee and obtain a decision in the matter. I had also spoken to the Deputy Chairman several times. I think it is important that there is clarity on the issue so that work can go forward.' Chidambaram also pointed out that 'some inspired stories have appeared in the media painting the MHA black and presenting distorted facts'. He requested the PM to instruct the Planning Commission to bring a note to cabinet and added that 'it would not be in the interest of the government to allow the controversy to be played out in the media'. The next day, the tone and text of the letter made it to the newspapers.[9]

Institutional conflicts come stapled with any new policy. Resolution of conflicts within government is frequently guided and crafted by the coming together of personalities, by induction of specialisation and political context. On 3 October, Pulok Chatterjee, perceived to be close to the Gandhi family, took over as the principal secretary to the prime minister, replacing T.K.A Nair, who went on to become adviser to PM. Chatterjee had just returned from the World Bank, where he was executive director. For more than a decade, the Bank had helped governments of countries, especially in Latin America, to develop conditional cash transfer programmes for alleviation of poverty, for direct payment of small subsidies to cover health, education, pension and access to food. In 2010, the World Bank had replicated the idea in seventeen countries.[10] Chatterjee was aware of the successes and pitfalls of cash benefit transfers. Also, having been in the PMO earlier, he knew the bureaucratic terrain and the political landscape.

Chatterjee met with Home Secretary R.K. Singh and RGI Chandramouli in November to understand the issues. They brainstormed, crafting solutions – the tangled arguments took more than a few weeks to untangle. A possible remedy was considered and a note was drafted. This was shared between the dramatis personae and their ministries. In January 2012, Manmohan Singh called Chidambaram and Pranab Mukherjee for a meeting for what he terms 'delicate intervention'.

Mukherjee carried with him a copy of *The Economist*, which on 17 November 2011 had described Aadhaar as 'India's identity revolution',[11] and then revisited the programme in its 14 January 2012 issue. The magazine said, 'For a country that fails to meet its most basic challenges – feeding the hungry, piping clean water, fixing roads – it seems incredible that India is rapidly building the world's biggest, most advanced, biometric database of personal identities.'[12] Reporting on the discourse around the project, it commented that while some of the resistance to the project 'was principled', much of it came from people who benefited from the patronage system. 'UID,' it said, 'would make this harder. That is why it faces such fierce opposition, and why it could transform India.'[13] Mukherjee, an avid consumer of news and information, had read the piece and shared it with Chidambaram and Manmohan Singh.

On 27 January, the cabinet committee on UIDAI met and cleared Phase III of the UIDAI project, allowing enrolment of 400 million more persons across eighteen states. The decision was announced in a press briefing by Chidambaram in the presence of Ahluwalia and Nilekani, to signal consensus and peace. The government declared that the 'NPR enrolment will continue as envisaged, but if in the course of enrolment, if a person indicates he/she is already enrolled for Aadhaar, the biometric data will not be captured by NPR. Instead, the Aadhaar number/enrolment number will be recorded in NPR and the biometric data will be sourced from the UIDAI. Detailed protocols will be worked out by the Inter Ministerial Coordination Committee (IMCC) already constituted by the Ministry of Home Affairs so as to smoothly implement this simultaneous effort.'[14]

To avoid duplication, the UID and NPR would exchange data, thereby ensuring that each one's members were enrolled in the other's programme at the back end.

•

Floundering due to the contradictions within the coalition and plagued by allegations of corruption, UPA II sought to push policies that would change the narrative back to the pro-poor plank the coalition had come to power on. It embarked on a two-pronged strategy to regain control over the political narrative.

One: a justiciable provision for food security to over 75 per cent of the rural population and up to 50 per cent of the urban population across the country. The idea was cleared by an empowered group of ministers in July 2011. Five kilograms of food grains per person per month would be supplied at subsidised prices of Rs 3/2/1 per kg for rice/wheat/coarse grains. After consultations with states, ministries and comments from stakeholders, a vetted version was cleared by the Union Cabinet of Ministers on 18 December 2011. On 22 December, the National Food Security Bill 2011 was introduced in the Lok Sabha amidst commotion over the Lok Pal Bill, which was being processed to meet with strident demands for an anti-corruption watchdog. The Opposition protested that these were diversionary tactics. The Bill was referred to the Parliamentary Standing Committee on Food, Consumer Affairs and Public Distribution. Pending that, the Ministry of Finance and the Ministry of Agriculture headed by Sharad Pawar conducted a series of meetings with states and with various departments.

Two: the strategy for the turnaround in political fortunes was to promote and propel the idea of direct cash benefit transfers: entitlements for education, health care and subsidies would be paid directly into the accounts of intended beneficiaries. It had crafted a political tag line too – *Aap ka paisa, aap ke haath* (Your money, in your hand).[15] The slogan was in tune with the 2004 slogan, Congress *ka haath aam aadmi ke saath* (The hand of the Congress, with the poor).

Direct Benefit Transfers or DBT, as it was called within government, was inspired by the success of such programmes in Latin America. It had political ballast. Congress scion Rahul Gandhi had been inspired by the work of Peruvian economist Hernando De Soto, who in 1986 had theorised about 'popular capitalism' in his book *The Other Path*. De Soto had evangelised the need for property rights and access to credit for the poor to rise above their circumstances. Rahul Gandhi had looked at the work done in cash transfers in Latin America – Bolsa Família in Brazil, Oportunidades in Mexico, Familias en Acción in Colombia et al – and felt it could be done in India too.

This created room for the Aadhaar-enabled cash transfer system. On 23 February, the Task Force on Aadhaar Enabled Unified Payment Infrastructure, led by Nilekani, submitted its report to the finance minister. It advocated the creation of a government e-payments gateway to release funds from MoF to ministries, an Aadhaar account opening and authentication platform, an Aadhaar payments bridge via NPCI which would enable transfer of funds into accounts on the basis of an Aadhaar number, creation of a micro ATM network that was interoperable – that is, usable by different

The Politics of Politics

players across systems – and introduction of banking services through mobile phones. Releasing the report, Finance Minister Mukherjee said the Aadhaar-enabled e-payment systems would go a long way 'in ensuring timely payments directly to beneficiaries' and in reducing costs and leakages.

All these ideas found traction. The Congress saw it as a win-win and the gateway to UPA III. The politics was pro-poor and the economics pro-reforms. The optics also promised reduction of corruption. Mukherjee announced in Budget 2012–13 that UIDAI had enrolled over 200 million persons and that 'The Aadhaar platform is now ready to support the payments of MG-NREGA; old age, widow and disability pensions; and scholarships directly to the beneficiary accounts in selected areas.'[16]

It was Mukherjee's last budget. The presidential polls were round the corner. His name had been among the frontrunners but it was not certain if the Congress would be willing to lose their chief crisis manager, by nominating him as president. On 13 June, Mamata Banerjee and Mulayam Singh suggested Manmohan Singh or Somnath Chatterjee for president. The Congress party announced Mukherjee as their candidate.[17] On 25 July 2012, Pranab Mukherjee was sworn in as the thirteenth president of India in the central hall of Parliament by Justice S.H. Kapadia, then chief justice of India.

The political environment, meanwhile, was deteriorating for the Congress-led UPA. The coal scam reared its head in March 2012, with a draft report of the CAG revealing that 'inefficient' allocation of coal blocks in 2004–2009 resulted in windfall gains to allottees and loss to the exchequer, estimated at Rs 10.7 trillion. Prime Minister Manmohan Singh, who had held the additional portfolio of coal for some time during the period, argued that 'the observations of the CAG are clearly disputable' and offered to quit public life if found guilty. Meanwhile, the CVC, based on complaints by two BJP MPs, Javadekar and Hansraj Ahir, directed a CBI enquiry. In the 2G scam, the Supreme Court, hearing a bunch of petitions, cancelled 122 licences granted during Raja's tenure and further directed auctioning of licences in four months' time.

By 2012, Manmohan Singh had become the longest-serving prime minister in the last twenty-five years. He was known to be an economist of stature, he had been finance minister when then Prime Minister Narasimha Rao – forced by a gargantuan economic crisis which had the country surreptitiously hocking its gold reserves – had opened India's economy to the world: the liberalisation of 1991. In this tenure, that reputation was coming undone and he was being held responsible for 'policy paralysis'.

Between 2007 and 2012, the government had underperformed on every index of infrastructure.[18] They were supposed to build 48,000 km of roads but delivered only on 17,000 km. They planned for 78000 MW of generating capacity and built 55,000, of which nearly 30,000 MW lay idle without fuel, despite a January

2012 commitment by the PMO. This was largely due to the civil war within the government, and differences of opinion on the trade-offs between growth and public good, between public projects and individual rights, on what constituted environmental protection, and how the problems of land acquisition could be resolved.

Add to this the growing perception that the political climate had turned hostile to foreign investors. The two signal events in this regard were the retrospective tax amendment following the Vodafone tax case and the controversy over intellectual property rights. The Economic Survey of 2012–13 quantified the general suspicion when it pointed out that investments worth more than Rs 7 trillion were stalled – in electricity, roads, telecommunication services, steel, real estate and mining projects.[19] Stalled investments represent not just loss of growth but endanger job creation.

Unsurprisingly, the economy was sliding into yet another crisis. Fiscal deficit for 2011–12 was 5.9 per cent and estimated at over 5 per cent for 2012–13 thanks to $100-plus crude oil prices plus rising food and fuel subsidies. The current account deficit, the gap between dollar inflows and outflows, was as bad as in 1991 – in pre-liberalised India – at 3.6 per cent. This was due in some measure due to poor exports, higher oil imports and a rise in gold imports. On the ground, inflation was rising, growth had slowed down.

In April, Standard and Poor's had changed its outlook on India from stable to negative and cautioned that political roadblocks to economic policymaking could put India at risk. In June, Fitch Ratings also revised its outlook from stable to negative. Moody's retained its rating but did express concern over fading investor confidence and worsening conditions. Manmohan Singh, who was holding additional charge of the Finance Ministry after Mukherjee stepped down, called for a 'revival of animal spirits' to reverse the climate of pessimism.[20]

P. Chidambaram took over as finance minister on 31 July 2012. He presented the worst-case scenarios to the party high command and said government must cut expenditure by at least a trillion rupees. A substantial part of this was going towards subsidising those who did not need it. These were not below or on the poverty line, yet they were availing government subsidies in the form of systemic leaks or largesse for food grains, cooking gas (LPG) and motor diesel. Public expenditure was ring-fenced into a corral of conditions to cut fiscal deficit, new duties were announced on gold imports; subsidies had to be targeted.

Aadhaar had new champions: Chidambaram and the state of the economy.

●

The context of a crisis seemed tailor-made for the idea of direct benefit transfers. Mysore in Karnataka already had a pilot project for selling LPG at market price, backed by a direct transfer of subsidy into the beneficiary account.

The Politics of Politics

A similar project for transfer of subsidy on kerosene into bank accounts was being tried in Alwar, Rajasthan. In Jharkhand, the Aadhaar platform had been used with success to validate PDS ration cards. The government began talking about how Aadhaar could be leveraged to reduce leakage.

In September, Manmohan Singh called a meeting of all ministries to set up the architecture for cash transfers leveraging Aadhaar. The move was presented 'as a major push to transfer individual benefits directly into the bank accounts of beneficiaries'. The prime minister announced the creation of a national ministerial committee that included various ministries, a national executive committee of heads of departments for coordination, an Implementation Mission to finalise operational design, a Cash Transfer Mission for tackling issues of technology and a financial inclusion committee. The logic, the government explained, 'was to cut down wastage, duplication and leakages and enhance efficiency'.[21] The plan was to expand cash transfer of subsidies to cover the entire population.

An enabler came to be soon enough. On 9 October, NPCI announced the launch of the Aadhaar-based remittance facility, leveraging its real-time payment platform to facilitate money transfer from one Aadhaar number to another or from an Aadhaar number to an account and vice versa on a 24x7 basis in a simple format. Participating in the initiative were ICICI Bank, Bank of Baroda, Union Bank of India, State Bank of India,

Maharashtra Cooperative Bank and the Mehsana Urban Cooperative Bank. The facility could be used for transfer of government benefits, to bring transparency, reduce delivery cost, expedite process and expand financial inclusion.

On a parallel track, the privacy issue seemed to be approaching a resolution. On 16 October, the Group of Experts on Privacy led by Justice Shah submitted its report – ninety-one pages, including a draft Bill – to Ashwani Kumar, minister of planning. The Shah Committee recommended a conceptual framework for the legislation on privacy. Recommendations included the following: a regulatory framework of privacy commissioners at the Central and regional levels, a system of co-regulation where self-regulation would be approved by the privacy commissioner.

It was mooted that individuals be given the choice to opt in or opt out, that is, have the choice of providing their Aadhaar number without fear of a service being denied. The committee recommended nine privacy principles and observed, 'The fundamental philosophy underlining the principles is the need to hold the data controller accountable for the collection, processing and use to which the data is put, thereby ensuring that the privacy of the data subject is guaranteed.'[22] Ashwani Kumar said a Privacy Act was necessary as, in a democracy, one had to ensure that 'no one right is so exercised so as to infringe upon the rights of individuals'.[23] A law was on the anvil. Or so it seemed then.

The Politics of Politics

Meanwhile, the stage was set for cash benefit transfers in India and it began with a political bang in Rajasthan. On 20 October, Dudu, a small tehsil in Ajmer Lok Sabha constituency, which was represented by Sachin Pilot, wore a festive look for the launch of the Aadhaar-enabled service. The who's who of the Congress – including Prime Minister Manmohan Singh, UPA Chairperson Sonia Gandhi, and Union ministers P. Chidambaram, C.P. Joshi, Namo Narain Meena, Ashwani Kumar and Mukul Wasnik – descended on the village from Delhi. The first beneficiaries, Lali Devi, Meera Devi, Banwari Lal and Birda Ram, received benefits under various welfare programmes such as Chief Minister's BPL Housing Scheme, Chief Minister's Higher Education Scholarship Scheme and MNREGA.

It was also the day Aadhaar enrolments crossed 210 million. Manmohan Singh lauded the UIDAI team and Nilekani and said, 'Today we will be giving the 21st crore Aadhaar number to a resident of Dudu here in Rajasthan and also launch the Aadhaar Enabled Service Delivery across the country so that benefits of various schemes reach residents.' Sonia Gandhi presented the political message: 'Aadhaar is the world's largest social inclusion programme. It was the dream of Rajivji that the power of technology be used for the benefit of Aam Admi. The Aadhaar programme is the next step of this dream.' Chidambaram declared, 'It is our aim that every resident should have an Aadhaar number. The poor will benefit the most from Aadhaar as the Government will be able to correctly identify beneficiaries of various social sector schemes based on the Aadhaar number. The ongoing pilots have also proved that Aadhaar is like a boon to beneficiaries.'[24]

The government simultaneously showcased the national reach and the potential of Aadhaar. Beneficiaries in Kakinada, Andhra Pradesh got their quota of ration using Aadhaar Online Authentication System; in Aurangabad in Maharashtra, payments under the Scholarship and Old Age Pension Social Security Welfare Scheme were made available through micro ATMs via the Aadhaar-enabled payment system; in Mysore, residents received LPG using a hand-held authenticating device; in Ramgarh district of Jharkhand, MGNREGS wages were transferred directly to accounts; and in West Tripura, payment of Old Age Pensions was Aadhaar enabled.

On his return to Delhi, Manmohan Singh accelerated Aadhaar's progress by creating a committee under Ahluwalia, Principal Secretary Pulok Chatterjee and the cabinet secretary. In November, the government announced a schedule for the national rollout – fifty-one districts by 1 January, eighteen states by 1 April 2013 and the rest of the states by 1 April 2014. There was a sense of urgency as the PM conducted preparedness meetings, and various ministries and the UIDAI conducted workshops on the how-to factors.

In November 2012, a study by the National Institute of Public Finance and Policy stated that 'Substantial benefits would accrue to the government by integrating

The Politics of Politics

Aadhaar with schemes such as PDS MGNREGS, fertiliser and LPG subsidies as well as housing, education and health programmes.' While this triggered a debate on the quantum of savings, the point that seemed to appeal to people was that Aadhaar could prevent diversion of their quota. This, and the possibility that the absence of Aadhaar could lead to being denied their quota, propelled enrolment.

Through all this, systemic issues continued to dog the implementation of Aadhaar. Members of Parliament were concerned that unverified data was being collected and raised national security concerns. In the Lok Sabha, member of Parliament K. Murugeshan Anandan asked the government if it was true that the 'Aadhaar project has come under the Intelligence Bureau scanner following several complaints that the Unique identity numbers have been issued in the name of fruits, vegetables like apple, coriander, etc.' The government admitted in response: 'The Home Ministry has raised the matter of integrity of the data collected by the UIDAI as well as its security in view of the methodology adopted by the UIDAI.' Minister of Planning Ashwani Kumar was at pains to clarify that the 'Aadhaar project is a developmental initiative and not a security related initiative.'

Shiv Sena MP Anandrao Adsul asked the government if it was true that 'unverified data was being collected by UIDAI; whether the creation of false profiles in the project may compromise internal security' and what steps were being taken by the government. Ashwani

Kumar clarified that UIDAI sought both proof of identity and proof of address documents. For those who did not have documents, the Demographic Data Standards and Verification Procedures Committee had provided a process where introducers such as elected officials, postmen, teachers or Aanganwadi/ASHA workers duly notified by registrars could validate applicants.

In mix-ups that caused much mirth and concern, Aadhaar cards were issued with photographs of empty chairs, trees and other inanimate objects. There were also cases where the enrolment operator's fingerprints were registered instead of the applicant's.[25] These errors were traced to operator carelessness and the cards were cancelled. At Umri in Bhind, an agency enrolled Tommy Singh, son of Sheru Singh, male, with the date of birth as 26/11/2009.[26] Tommy Singh's photograph revealed he was the house pet of one of the supervisors at the agency. Tommy's owner was arrested. The matter came to light when people complained to the police that, while they were having trouble getting enrolled, dogs and other animals were registered for Aadhaar numbers. In another instance, 369 Aadhaar letters were found in a drain in Faridabad. The matter was raised in Parliament by H.D. Chavan, BJP MP from Maharashtra. An enquiry revealed that the postman had left his bicycle unattended, along with the Aadhaar letters. The bicycle was reportedly stolen.

There were human foibles and idiocies, errors in process. And there was outright fraud. In March

The Politics of Politics

2013, the government informed the Lok Sabha that UIDAI had to cancel 384,000 Aadhaar numbers – over 230,000 from Andhra Pradesh alone.[27] Operators had sought to scam the system using an enabling provision for inclusion. Under the 'biometric exception clause' they could enrol people with biometric exceptions. The rule said: 'If the resident has any deformities due to which it is not possible to take fingerprints/iris, these also have to be captured as a biometric exception.' That is, the exception photograph showing the resident's face and both limbs must be taken irrespective of type of exception.[28]

Operators in Andhra Pradesh, Delhi, Tamil Nadu, Maharashtra, Odisha, Jharkhand, Tripura and Uttar Pradesh had tried to exploit this loophole by using permutations and combinations of photos with faces and limbs. The authorities were alerted when 45,000 Aadhaar letters came back undelivered in Andhra Pradesh. The back-end of UIDAI has a mechanism to audit enrolment agencies. One of the audit parameters (among many, including who did how many enrolments) was use of the exception clause. A review revealed that operators who were meant to first try for fingerprint impressions and only then use the exception clause, were manipulating provisions to notch higher number of enrolments and fees. These operators were identified, and 384,000 out of the 410,000 cards issued under the exception clause were cancelled.

In June 2013, UIDAI also had to issue a cautionary

notice warning people against approaching enterprising touts who could dupe them or issue fake Aadhaar cards.

Activism against the Aadhaar programme also picked up pace during this period. On Friday, 30 November 2012, the Supreme Court issued a notice to the Union government on a PIL against the implementation of Aadhaar while a Bill was pending in Parliament.[29] A bench of Chief Justice Altamas Kabir and Justice J. Chelameswar issued notice on a public interest litigation filed by Justice K.S. Puttaswamy, a retired judge of the Karnataka High Court. The petition said the decision to implement the scheme was an attempt to circumvent parliamentary discussion and the process of legislation.

There was also, as it would be later revealed, for Aadhaar, a significant political development. On 20 December, Gujarat Chief Minister Narendra Modi scored a hat-trick as he led the BJP to victory in the Gujarat Assembly polls. Jubilant workers had only one slogan at the party office and in Hindi – 'Gujarat to jhaanki hai, Dilli abhi baaki hai' (Gujarat is only a trailer, Delhi is the big picture). At the victory rally, Modi spoke not in Gujarati but in Hindi. He knew he was being beamed live across India. This win, he said, was for people who wanted India to prosper. As the crowd chanted 'PM, PM' and 'Delhi, Delhi' Modi quipped, 'If you all insist I will visit Delhi on December 27 for a day.'

The Politics of Politics

It was a clarion call, as much for the Congress as for those running the BJP in Delhi and those in its advisory body, the Rashtriya Swayamsevak Sangh (RSS).

It was not the defeat in Gujarat that was the issue for the Congress – it had been out of power in the state since 1989. The real worry was Modi's emergence as a national challenger.[30]

The Congress scrambled about to regain political relevance. It decided to focus on bottom of the pyramid politico-economics, beginning with getting the law on food security passed. With it they would further push direct benefit transfers. In January 2013, the parliamentary standing committee submitted its report on the new food security law with clause by clause recommendations and asked the Central government to consult state governments. Faced with a blockade in Parliament, desperate for optics and a handle, the government promulgated an Ordinance for food security in July. The law was eventually enacted in September 2013. The government put Aadhaar on the fast track to expand enrolment and gain mass allegiance.

The Congress' big idea was to make Aadhaar a symbol of empowerment. This called for expansion of Aadhaar across sectors, for the unique identity card to be made ubiquitous in usage. The government expanded the use of Aadhaar as a valid document for access to services. Rajeev Shukla, minister of planning, described Aadhaar in the Rajya Sabha as 'soft identity infrastructure which can be used to reengineer public services so that these lead to efficient and better delivery of services'.[31] He added that state and Central government ministries had been advised to leverage Aadhaar as a platform for access and delivery.

In a series of executive actions, the government made Aadhaar a valid document for proof of identity and proof of address. It could be used for obtaining mobile phone connections and LPG connections, for registration of vehicles, for rail travel, for voting in the absence of voter ID cards, for obtaining a driving licence and for access to medical treatment at government hospitals under specific schemes. The governments of Sikkim, Tripura, Andhra Pradesh, Jammu and Kashmir, Chandigarh, Nagaland, Haryana, Manipur and Rajasthan recognised Aadhaar as a valid document for various resident schemes. The government also pushed for recognition of Aadhaar for obtaining passports and for the Permanent Account Number issued for income tax filings.

One big challenge in combining Aadhaar and DBT to trigger a multiplier effect was the stark reality that over two-thirds of Indians did not have a bank account. The Finance Ministry nudged the Reserve Bank of India and public sector banks to accept Aadhaar to open accounts. This gave the financial inclusion programme a significant push: a major share of the 130 million new accounts opened during UPA I and UPA II were enabled by Aadhaar. The expansion of DBT required access not just to accounts but to money. The Finance Ministry enabled this by recognising Aadhaar based eKYC – instant authentication for all financial services.

The Politics of Politics

In March 2013, the government expanded the ambit of direct benefit transfers of subsidies. Manmohan Singh told the National Committee on DBT in April, 'We cannot afford to fail. We need to show that we can deliver results and benefits.'[32] The committee expanded the use of Aadhaar-based DBT to twenty-six schemes. Aadhaar was made mandatory to access LPG subsidies first in twenty districts, then to 291 districts, in phases covering 100 million consumers. Petroleum marketing companies pinged the phones of consumers with SMS messages, telling them to get an Aadhaar number and link it to their LPG number and bank accounts.

Nilekani recalls with a grin, 'Suddenly all sorts of people from film stars to my neighbour, an MP, began calling, worried about their kitchens.' The launch of DBT for LPG catalysed Aadhaar enrolments, put it on steroids in a sense. In thirty-one days in July, UIDAI recorded 20 million enrolments. To put this in perspective, it had taken UIDAI 106 days to enrol the first million. On 17 August, UIDAI announced that enrolments had crossed the 400 million mark.[33]

The Congress decided that it would use entitlements and cash transfers as a plank in the forthcoming elections. However, events overtook intent. On 23 September, the Supreme Court took up the PIL filed by Justice Puttaswamy and other similar petitions against Aadhaar. A bench of Justices B.S. Chauhan and S.A. Bobde in a brief order stated, 'No person should suffer for not getting the Aadhaar card in spite of the fact that some authority had issued a circular making it mandatory and when any person applies to get the Aadhaar card voluntarily, it may be checked whether that person is entitled for it under the law and it should not be given to any illegal immigrant.'[34]

The order left the Congress nonplussed and emboldened the Opposition. MPs raised the issue in Parliament and asked whether the issue of Aadhaar had legal validity post the order. This put the government on a sticky wicket. It knew in January 2009 that UIDAI needed legal cover. Yet, till September 2013, UIDAI lacked statutory status. On 7 November, the government announced that a new updated Bill, the National Identification Authority Bill 2013, would be introduced in the winter session of parliament.[35] The session was a washout. PRS Legislative, a research institute that tracks the functioning of the Indian Parliament and works with MPs across political parties, put it in perspective when it pointed out, 'Lok Sabha worked for 4 hours and 31 minutes, that is, six per cent of the scheduled time and Rajya Sabha for 11 hours and 24 minutes or 19 per cent of the scheduled time.'[36]

Politics was in poll mode. On 8 December, results for the elections to four states delivered Congress a sucker punch. It lost Delhi, a state where it had been in power for fifteen years, and Rajasthan. It couldn't make any dent in Madhya Pradesh and Chhattisgarh, where Shivraj Chauhan and Raman Singh returned to power for a third term. In Rajasthan, where it had enacted a law to guarantee delivery of public services within a stipulated time[37] and where the Congress-led UPA had launched the Direct Benefit of Transfers, the Congress won just twenty-one of the 200 seats in the State Assembly.

This thrashing in the Assembly elections brought up the schism within the party. Internal murmurs against the Aadhaar programme acquired decibel power. The decision to impose an arbitrary cap and the confusion that ensued reflected the disconnect between the party, the government and the people, particularly the urban middle class. The Opposition leveraged this wedge. BJP Mahila Morcha members led the protests against capping of LPG and linking of Aadhaar with subsidies. Activists protested that the mandatory linkage of Aadhaar to LPG subsidies was a violation of the September 2013 Supreme Court order.

Within the Congress, MPs and MLAs built pressure on the government to halt the DBT programme. On 27 January, the matter came up in the parliamentary estimates committee, which oversees efficiency of government and efficacy of policies. Its chairman, Francisco Sardinha, a Congressman, and other MPs, called for the scrapping of the DBT scheme of LPG cylinders. Three days later, on 30 January, at the Cabinet Committee on Political Affairs, Defence Minister A.K. Antony and Food Minister K.V. Thomas asked that the linkage of Aadhaar and LPG subsidies be suspended and the newly imposed cap of nine cylinders per year be removed.[38]

On 4 February 2014, Aadhaar enrolments touched 570 million. On that day, the Cabinet Committee on UIDAI met to approve the next phase of Aadhaar enrolments.[39] It was decided that UIDAI would expand its operations to Uttar Pradesh, Bihar, Chhattisgarh and Uttarakhand, and carry out the enrolment exercise in addition to enrolment carried out by the registrar general of India.

The decision was put on pause, though. The government bowed to the political voice of the party. Manmohan Singh says, 'There was a perception among some senior leaders in the party that there should be a review of the programme of Direct Benefit Transfer of subsidies for LPG. They felt that this would harm the prospects of the party in the polls.' He directed the formation of an eleven-member committee to review the programme of direct transfer of subsidies for LPG. The DBT for LPG was suspended. Aadhaar was presented by the UPA as a solution in 2009. Five years later, senior leaders of the party saw the solution as a problem. UIDAI's expansion came to a halt.

7

Modification

PM MAKES IDENTITY THE PRIME PLATFORM

By February 2014, India had contracted election fever. The Election Commission (EC) called for a meeting with all political parties on 4 February to discuss scheduling polls across India in 543 constituencies. In a large country like India, the EC had many considerations to take into account: the newly contoured constituencies post delimitation, holidays, school exams, the availability of security forces and the weather.

It was only a matter of days before it was curtains for UPA II. Like a team scrambling for runs in the slog overs of a cricket match, Congress ministers were panting to paint up and post their performances for public favour. It was rush hour for announcements and inaugurations – conversion into six lanes of a highway in Madhya Pradesh, revival of stalled road projects in Goa, Kerala and Maharashtra, bio gas projects for cooking, inauguration of AIMS in Rishikesh, and so on and so forth.

On 17 February, Finance Minister P. Chidambaram presented the interim budget and made a valiant effort to downplay the oft-repeated charge of policy paralysis.[1] It was a data parade on ten years of UPA. 'Ten years ago, we produced 213 million tonnes of food grains; today, we produce 263 million tonnes of food grains. Ten years ago, the installed power capacity was 112,700 MW; today, it is 234,600 MW. Ten years ago, there were 51,511 km of rural roads under PMGSY; today, we have 389,578 km. Ten years ago, the Central Government's expenditure on education was Rs 10,145 crore; this year, we allocated Rs 79,451 crore. Ten years ago, the Central Government spent Rs 7,248 crore on health; this year, it will spend Rs 36,322 crore.'

Chidambaram also listed Direct Benefit Transfer as a highlight. A quick recap of that section of the budget speech: money was being transferred to beneficiaries under twenty-seven schemes, 5.42 million transactions had been put through and Rs 33.7 billion had been transferred as LPG subsidy to beneficiaries. He did admit, however, that the scheme had been put on hold even as he reiterated the need for it and the party's commitment to it.

It was a tough sell given the perception of atrophy in the party and in the government. And the legislative record said it all. It had passed the law for a Lok Pal but kept the critical bills on benami transactions, public procurement and whistle-blowers pending for five years. UPA had waxed eloquent about delivery of services but couldn't get the law for time-bound delivery

Modification

or the grievance redressal through. The UPA's record on pushing legislation, for reforms and for change, in Parliament, was rather indefensible – thirty-eight bills were allowed to lapse, twenty bills were passed in one house and not in the other, and 107 bills were listed as pending. Even though the Congress improved its tally from 145 to 206 in 2009, UPA had not thrived, merely survived.

On 5 March 2014, the Election Commission announced the schedule for the 2014 polls. They were to be held in nine phases between 7 April and 12 May with the results to be announced on 16 May 2014.[2]

The BJP was ready for the announcement. Waiting in the wings was three-time Gujarat Chief Minister Narendra Modi. The strategy was already in place. The strapline was Congress-Mukt Bharat (Congress-free – by implication, corruption-free – country), the overarching theme was of a Can-do Sarkar.

The Gujarat CM was presented as a doer, an able administrator, and was projected as a person who could change the face of India as he had done in Gujarat. The BJP–RSS combine presented the Modi-model, a promise of solutions blended with the Bharatiya pride factor.

Modi was the party, Modi was the manifesto, Modi was the campaigner and Modi symbolised it all. The campaign slogan unsurprisingly was 'Ab ki baar Modi sarkar' (This time, Modi).

Mission 272-plus was planned down to the commas and dots. It was managed by people who were consulted, instructed and informed about exactly what had to be done, how it had to be done, when, where, by whom. The team included tech whiz Rajesh Jain, who landscaped the data across constituencies; Prashant Kishor, who led a group called Citizens for Accountable Governance; Hiren Joshi, an officer in the Gujarat chief minister's office; tech entrepreneur B.G. Mahesh; industrialist Surendra Patel and Modi's close aides, Gujarat Resident Commissioner Bharath Lal and Arvind Sharma who steered the Vibrant Gujarat summits, as also people drafted from media and films, right-wing intellectuals and writers.

The BJP's 2014 mission-Modi manifesto did not mince words. It was well crafted and got the political syntax just right. It listed as imperatives for focus and resolution: price rise, poor delivery of goods, unemployment, corruption and black money, and policy paralysis. In crisp bullet points, it hinted at the solutions. Interestingly, an earlier draft by party seniors, in the usual yada-yada style, was overhauled by Modi's core group to make it modern. The idea was to appeal to a new generation of voters and those who sought change. It said, 'The biggest challenge that India faces today is to restore the credibility of, and trust in the Union Government. In recent years, the Union Government has lost every semblance of credibility. Its intentions, integrity and initiatives, all are questionable. The Congress party has not only lowered the dignity of the Government, but also the dignity of India.' The manifesto promised, 'We will ensure that the chain of responsibility and accountability is built in the system.'

Modification

Social media was leveraged alongside a media strategy in the manner of a blockbuster release, unprecedented in the history of Indian elections. The internet was pepper-sprayed with messaging to create affinity with the like-minded, techies used algorithms to track feedback. Mission 272-plus brought into play communication, connectivity, strategy, tactics, technology and sheer political entrepreneurship. The front pages of all major newspapers in all languages were booked very much in advance with ads for the prime candidate and released with time-capsule precision. In comparison, the Congress campaign was stuck in the Stone Age.

Modi himself employed technology while addressing meetings. Holograms caught everyone's attention, as did large backlit screens, video clusters of 'chai pe charcha' (conversations over a glass of tea), since a back-story had given the man an up-from-tea-seller-to-putative-PM halo.

All of this had multiplier effects in the bricks-and-mortar media, which fuelled the internet cycle to trend on social media. NaMo, as he came to be called, dressed crisply and ensured he provided contrasts for the cameras, presenting his best profile as he engaged with communities of interest. His content varied depending upon the geography, the audience and their state-specific aspirations, even as he wooed them with the idea of Shrestha Bharat (a great India).

Modi's travels, campaign speeches and interviews to the media were timed and designed to address each of the nine phases that went to polls, and ensured that his speeches were beamed live by channels which took his message into constituencies and him right into the homes of those about to cast their vote. Going direct to people via live streams and television disenfranchised the establishment media and gave Modi uninterrupted engagement with the voter; no loss in transmission by the intrusive ifs and buts of the print media on Gujarat.

Modi and the Mission Men were also not dependent on the party machinery to deliver the goods. They worked with the party for its participation and cooperation but the campaign was equally a message to those established within the party. There was close monitoring of both optics and outcomes – the messaging had to stay focussed on development.

•

In March 2014 Nilekani quit UIDAI and joined the Congress Party. On 8 March, the Congress released its first list of 184 candidates for the Lok Sabha polls.[3] It included Sonia Gandhi, Rahul Gandhi and the likes of Union ministers Salman Khurshid, Sriprakash Jaiswal, Sushilkumar Shinde, Milind Deora, Priya Dutt and Meira Kumar. Also on that first list was Nandan Nilekani, candidate for Bengaluru South.

The nomination made Nilekani and Aadhaar a target for the BJP and its leaders. Already, the BJP had made its view of the Aadhaar programme abundantly clear: in its opposition in Parliament, in television debates and in blogs and social media. Arun Jaitley, Leader of the Opposition in the Rajya Sabha, had blogged on the issue of privacy: 'The Government has

Modification

recently made the existence of the Aadhaar number as a condition precedent for undertaking several activities; from registering marriages to execution of property documents. Will those who encroach upon the affairs of others be able to get access to bank accounts and other important details by breaking into the system? If this ever becomes possible the consequences would be far messier.'[4]

Party spokesperson Meenakshi Lekhi said in Bengaluru that the Aadhaar project was 'dangerous' and also 'posed a threat to the country's security' as it regularised the stay of illegal immigrants at the cost of the welfare of genuine residents. 'Aadhaar needs a re-look to see if anything has gone wrong and to know who stores and shares the biometric data of citizens,' she said.[5] Rajeev Chandrashekar, Rajya Sabha MP, who launched BPL Mobile and owned a media house, in a signed article said, 'Aadhaar in its current form, is a house of cards and resting primarily on hype, and will surely not achieve any of the laudable objectives of eradicating corruption. This will become obvious to many, as the layers of hype are peeled off and the stark reality becomes obvious.'[6]

Less than a fortnight away from polling, on 24 March 2014, the Supreme Court, while hearing a matter related to sharing of biometric data for investigations, directed the government to withdraw notifications making Aadhaar mandatory. A bench of Justices B.S. Chauhan and J. Chelameswar told Solicitor General Mohan Parasaran that, despite the earlier order directing the Centre not to insist on Aadhaar cards, there were several complaints that the authorities were insisting on them for providing benefits. Justice Chauhan told Parasaran: 'I have received a lot of letters which say that Aadhaar card is mandatory despite court orders. We had already passed orders saying no one should suffer for not having Aadhaar card. How can you insist on Aadhaar card? If there are any instructions that Aadhaar is mandatory, it should be withdrawn immediately.'[7]

In Bengaluru, Ananth Kumar, who Nilekani was contesting against, charged at a public interaction that data collected by UIDAI was 'passed on to America'. He demanded that the government stop issuing Aadhaar cards.[8] Campaigning in Bengaluru, Rajnath Singh, then the BJP president, declared, 'We will review Aadhaar project if BJP-led NDA comes to power and look into its flaws. Instead of Aadhaar, National Population Register should be the basis of distributing direct cash benefits to targeted people.'[9]

Narendra Modi, the BJP's prime ministerial candidate in 2014, tweeted from his handle @narendramodi: 'On Aadhaar, neither the Team that I met, nor PM could answer my Qs on security threat it can pose. There is no vision, only political gimmick.'[10] Modi also recalled raising the issue with Prime Minister Manmohan Singh. 'At the National Security Council meeting, I asked the Prime Minister to study questions I raised on Aadhaar. I said the scheme would not work if questions are not addressed.'[11]

The writing on the wall read like Aadhaar's obituary—if the BJP were to come to power.

Modification

The results came in on 16 May. It wasn't a Modi wave, it was virtually a tsunami. Nearly every electoral record had been ground into dust by the Modi juggernaut; the BJP and its allies rode to a massive victory with 336 seats. The BJP polled 31 per cent of the votes and won 282 seats, a gain of 166 over its 2009 tally. It was the first party to win a majority in the Lok Sabha since 1984. The BJP and its allies had won seventy-one seats in Uttar Pradesh, India's most populous state, again a record. Narendra Modi won both the seats he contested, in Gujarat and in Uttar Pradesh.

The Congress won just forty-four seats – its lowest tally ever. Of the 464 candidates who contested on a Congress ticket, 178 forfeited their deposits.[12] Sanjay Nirupam of the Congress, who lost from Mumbai North, defined the defeat of the Congress: 'Even Narendra Modi would have badly lost in the Lok Sabha elections had he contested on a Congress ticket.'[13] Nilekani lost to Ananth Kumar.

The Modi Sarkar took charge of the reins of the world's largest democracy on 26 May 2014. The swearing in saw everybody who was somebody in India's political, entertainment, sports and corporate world in attendance – one attendee quipped that more than half the market capitalisation of BSE Sensex was present. Also in attendance were heads of state from the neighbourhood and international dignitaries. Victory notwithstanding, the show had just started. The website of the prime minister, http://www.pmindia.gov.in, went live within seconds of Modi's swearing in.[14] In the Modi

Sarkar, communication mattered – it was a critical tool for narrative management.

It didn't take long for the government to put UIDAI and Aadhaar on the review radar. On 29 May, soon after taking charge, Home Minister Rajnath Singh hinted at the possibility of a merger of the National Population Register exercise and the Aadhaar scheme.[15] Officials of the Home Ministry suggested that the registrar general of India, who was in charge of the NPR exercise, would get back to the home minister with a detailed presentation suggesting the marriage of NPR and Aadhaar.

In May 2014, Ram Sewak Sharma, who had moved from UIDAI in March 2013 on promotion as chief secretary of Jharkhand, was brought back to head the Department of Electronics and Information Technology (DEIT). On 16 June, the National Informatics Centre, UIDAI and DIET organised a Workshop on Aadhaar Enabled e-Gov Applications & Services. Among those listed on the agenda were Dr Rajendra Kumar, JS (e-Gov), DeitY; Rajiv Gauba, in-charge of e-Gov; UIDAI chief Dr Vijay Madan; R.S. Sharma, secretary, Deity; Y.K. Sharma, adviser e-Gov; and Sujata Chaturvedi DDG, UIDAI.[16]

The workshop was part of a routine review of programmes – e-governance and, by extension, Aadhaar-enabled services – under the Ministry of Electronics and Information Technology. Departments, including UIDAI, made presentations, followed by a brainstorming session. This raised several eyebrows within the government, among political meteorologists in the bureaucracy and within the political establishment. It was scarcely a secret that the new government was all set to dismantle UIDAI and merge it with the NPR under the registrar general of India in the Home Ministry. The political incorrectness was noted.

From 1 June, Prime Minister Modi had set a scorching pace in government. His approach to administration was focussed on knowing who could deliver and inducting know-how. He was methodical in his assessment of the landscape, moves were made only after aligning priorities and pace to fit his own calculus. As was his wont, he called for a review of all the programmes and plans under each ministry. The DEIT was called on 23 June. Sharma had put together a compact presentation on what could be done. Since Sharma knew of Modi's interest in technology induction, he had included points on what could be done with the capacity and capability available for promoting e-governance.

Modi is constantly looking for technology solutions, not just for processes but also to engender a change in work culture. As PM, one of his first missives to his ministers was to declutter offices because they gave government a bad name and reflected poorly on India.[17] He also wanted to enforce punctuality at work and end delinquency among government officials, who tended to turn up in office late. This was not as easy as decluttering offices; it required enforcement.

As chief secretary in the government of Jharkhand, Sharma had set up a system whereby government officials needed to clock in using an Aadhaar-enabled biometric attendance system. He then put up the collated data on the Jharkhand government website. A dashboard displayed real-time information on the number of registered users, number of active users, number of persons in office, average time at which most officials clocked in and the average time at which they left.[18] This information was further disaggregated to reflect the Secretariat, for government institutions like hospitals, cooperative banks, schools and district offices.

Senior officers in the Prime Minister's Office had told Modi about the Jharkhand dashboards when he had first spoken about the need to enforce punctuality in government offices. Thereafter, he had been shown printouts and a demonstration. So, before Sharma could even start on his department presentation in June, Modi asked about Jharkhand's Aadhaar-enabled attendance system. Sharma spelt out the technology and the processes. Modi asked a few questions on how it could be bettered. Then he asked Sharma, 'Can you implement this system for all Central government offices?' Sharma said, 'Yes.' 'How long will it take to install,' asked the PM. Sharma replied, 'By end September.'

Prime Minister Narendra Modi instructed his secretary and Sharma, 'This must be done.'[19]

Sharma's presentation included the subject of e-governance, the entire architecture of UIDAI, the promise of Aadhaar and its potential to save billions of rupees for the government. He mentioned that 'even if government could reduce leakage and theft by 10 per cent it would be a big sum'.

Modification

When Sharma left the PMO, he saw a ray of hope. The PM's acceptance of the Aadhaar-enabled attendance system could yet save the entire project.

•

Around the end of June, Nilekani and his wife Rohini, who runs a social foundation, were vacating their Delhi residence on Safdarjang Lane, packing up to return to their Bengaluru base. They invited Sharma for lunch.

Over lunch Sharma told Nilekani about his presentation to the PM and the response to it. Nilekani was happy to hear this and thanked Sharma for the effort. Then Sharma said, 'Why don't you go and meet the Prime Minister? Aadhaar is your idea; it has so much potential, why don't you make this last attempt for it?' Rohini agreed. Like Sharma, she thought it couldn't possibly do any harm.

Nilekani found himself on the horns of a dilemma. On the one hand, he had lost the election on a Congress ticket and there was the history of campaign rhetoric, all the stuff that had been said. On the other, 'the thought that Aadhaar could be irretrievably shut down was heart-breaking'.

Nilekani had spoken with friends in government. He then met with Arun Jaitley, now finance minister. Jaitley advised him to meet the prime minister. Unlike in the UPA, and in other governments, back channels were not advisable. Back-channels are those intermediaries who carry a viewpoint to the top. Modi was known to have an aversion for back-channels; both RSS and BJP party bigwigs knew this. Modi owned and Modi ran the Modi Sarkar.

On 28 June, Nilekani telephoned the PMO and sought time on 1 July. He said that he would be in Delhi only for a day and would it be possible for him to meet the PM in the first part of that day. He was given an appointment for noon, 1 July, at South Block, the office of the prime minister.

It was a one-on-one meeting. In those thirty minutes, Nilekani outlined the potential of Aadhaar. 'I explained the platform, its expansion across many states, the applications that had been developed, the possibilities recommended by task forces and committees.' The PM had a clear understanding of the technology and had questions about migrants and the status of cases in the courts. Nilekani allayed the fears around data security and verification. He pointed to the low cost at which the platform had been developed. He underlined the fact that Aadhaar as a platform 'could help resolve many issues, including the targeting of subsidies and curbing corruption. It could lead to huge savings to the exchequer.' He also emphasised the need for an early passage of the UIDAI Bill in Parliament.

Modi met Nilekani on Tuesday. On Thursday, the Home Ministry was preparing to merge UIDAI and NPR, following a meeting with Rajnath Singh, IT, Telecom and Law Minister Ravi Shankar Prasad and Planning Minister Rao Inderjeet Singh.[20]

On Saturday, 5 July, Prime Minister Modi revived Aadhaar.

Modification

This followed a meeting with Jaitley and Rajnath Singh, attended by officials of the UIDAI, Home Ministry, Planning Commission and the PMO. A committee was formed to look into the issues. Modi asked Finance Minister Jaitley, the legal luminary in the government, to look into legal issues since there were cases pending in the Supreme Court. He also called for the revival of the National Identification Authority of India Bill that had been trashed by the Yashwant Sinha-led parliamentary standing committee.[21]

Prime Minister Modi, when asked by this author, about the revival of Aadhaar and his earlier criticism of it, says, 'The need for a common identity card was felt since the Vajpayee government was in power. A group of ministers even worked on this. However, not much was done during UPA I to carry forward this vision. Eventually Aadhaar was launched only in the second term of the UPA government.'

According to the prime minister, 'When Aadhaar was launched there were multiple issues and inadequacies with it. They simply could not envisage it holistically as an empowering mechanism for the masses. For them, It was just another scheme. I had suggested many ideas but the UPA regime simply didn't want to accept any suggestions from Narendra Modi.'

Elaborating on his party's earlier opposition, Modi says, 'Our problem was not with the idea of Aadhaar, but with the inadequacies of Aadhaar. We have never opposed anything for the sake of opposition. I do not believe in that kind of politics. The UPA government had a problem of imagination and an even bigger problem of implementation. I knew Aadhaar had potential. For years they ran Aadhaar, but it still didn't have any parliamentary backing, nor integration with public service delivery.'

Explaining how his government took it forward, the prime minister adds, 'We took a decision to separate the security issues that were raised by home ministry from the issue of Direct Benefit Transfer. We created a committee to look into the legal and technology issues, and we fixed it. We expanded the scope of Aadhaar, amplified the scale and augmented the speed. In a short span of time, the country has already saved about Rs 50,000 crores due to Aadhaar-based systems.'

I.G. Patel, in his 2002 book *Glimpses of Indian Economic Policy*, illuminates the interconnect between policy and political styles with a pen sketch of the leaders of his time. He says of former Prime Minister Indira Gandhi, 'There was nothing basically ideological about Mrs Gandhi. Everything was as it suited her at the time.' Her politics and the policies she pursued bear out this assessment.

In 1966, Indira Gandhi pushed through the biggest devaluation of the rupee, by over 57 per cent, in the quest for aid and loans from IMF and World Bank. For this, she didn't shy away from meeting with Lyndon Johnson, then the US president. Her approach towards nationalisation of banks, in 1969, was driven by the need of the economy – to aggregate public savings for popular programmes, deny political space to her opponents from

Modification

the Congress Syndicate and to entice the Left to support her. To further the cause of consolidation, she banned privy purses for the royalty, brought in tighter rules on monopolies (Monopolies and Restrictive Trade Practices Act) and cramped investment by multinationals. She also signed a friendship treaty with the Soviet Union. The same Mrs Gandhi, then went on to meet with US President Ronald Reagan in Cancun, Mexico, in 1981, and subsequently signed a technology agreement and opened up trade with the United States. She also signed agreements with France and UK for defence purchases of Mirage and Jaguar planes.

Narendra Modi is not bound by conventional definitions of ideology. His approach is based on political entrepreneurship, and policy is essentially an instrument to consolidate and expand political subscription. During his campaign, he had asked why government should be making railway coaches. The government has no business to be in business, he said. This led many to expect the dismantling of the public sector structure. One of his campaign slogans was minimum government maximum governance – many read this as a promise to shrink government.

Modi invests a lot of faith in the use of technology – for politics and for public policy. As the chief minister of Gujarat, his favourite haunt, when he had the time, was the Bhaskaracharya Institute for Space Applications and Geo-Informatics. Under him the Gujarat government harnessed space technology to propel groundwater management by using data to pinpoint where water bodies could be created, and for an SMS service telling fishermen where schools of fish were located and for how long. Digitisation and CCTV were used to improve octroi and other tax collection and curb corruption. There was also the push for renewables, canal-top solar projects and wind farms.

For Modi, therefore, Aadhaar was about using technology, a means to empower outcomes. He had issues with the Congress but had not allowed them to come in the way of Aadhaar enrolment in Gujarat. Instead, in 2011, he crafted the policy for a Modified Aadhaar-KYR Plus. There was also political context. The BJP manifesto described the promise to restore the economy to health as the 'Immediate Imperative'. Modi Sarkar rode to power on the slogan-chant *Achhe Din Ayenge* (Good days will come, somewhat like Reagan's 'Good Morning America'). Fiscal deficit, post the slashing of expenditure in 2013–14, was still very high at 4.5 per cent of GDP. This was being funded by loans – gross government borrowing had shot up from Rs 4.3 trillion to Rs 5.6 trillion between 2010 and 2014. Higher borrowings had pushed interest payments from Rs 2.3 trillion to Rs 4.2 trillion. In 2013–14, the government borrowed Rs 15.42 billion per day and paid Rs 11.69 billion per day towards interest payments.[22] The rise in borrowings was fuelled by a rise in subsidies, from Rs 1.73 trillion to Rs 2.55 trillion ; the government was spending Rs 7 billion per day on subsidies. Just the bill for fuel subsidies hovered between Rs 850 billion and Rs 960 billion.

Modification

The rise in fuel subsidies was driven by a rise in global oil prices since 2011, when it crossed US$100 per barrel – the UPA, cornered by corruption and inflation, couldn't hike prices. In July 2014, when Nilekani met with Modi and Aadhaar was revived, Brent Crude Oil prices were hovering around US$110 per barrel. Organisation of Petroleum Exporting Countries (OPEC) reports observed that bets by speculators had hit a record high, thanks to geopolitical tension in the Middle East:[23] the fall of Mosul to the Islamic State, the potential for escalation and US intervention in the civil war in Syria and attacks in Gaza. Forecasts didn't hold much hope that prices would come down. For Modi, Aadhaar's DBT afforded a way for migration to a new subsidy system that would bring down government expenditure.

On 9 July, the government tabled the Economic Survey for the year. The survey, said Jaitley, 'shows the gravity of the economic situation'.[24] It cautioned that cutting capital expenditure was not the route to cut fiscal deficit, underlined that 'Ill-targeted subsidies cramp the fiscal space for public investment and distort allocation of resources' and argued the need for rationalisation of subsidies.[25] In his speech presenting Budget 2014–15, Jaitley announced, 'I propose to overhaul the subsidy regime, including food and petroleum subsidies, and make it more targeted while providing full protection to the marginalized, poor and SC/STs. A new urea policy would also be formulated.'[26]

A few days before the new government took over, the

committee appointed in February by the Manmohan Singh regime for the 'Review of Direct Benefit Transfer for LPG Scheme' had submitted its report. The committee stated that 'the DBTL scheme was successful in achieving its objectives, viz. reducing diversion, eliminating ghost/ duplicate connections, and improving LPG availability.'[27] It also presented evidence: that a combination of self-selection with consumers opting out of LPG subsidy and the seeding of accounts with Aadhaar numbers was creating savings for the government.[28]

The primary requirement for conditional cash transfers to work is a bank account. For the government to be able to transfer subsidies via DBT, the consumer needs to have an account – this dictated ramping up of financial inclusion. On 31 July, Finance Minister Jaitley, addressing a meeting of CEOs of public sector banks and financial institutions, announced that the government would be launching a new programme of financial inclusion in 'Mission Mode' to provide households with facilities of savings, credit, remittances, insurance and pension.[29] There were 75 million households in the country that did not have a bank account and the government's target was that every village should get a banking facility within a reasonable distance and that every household should have at least one bank account within the time frame of one year.

The government could have leveraged technology to create a virtual bank. It could have converted the 12-digit Aadhaar number into a bank account number, defined it

Modification

as an Aadhaar account in the cloud, and allowed people to choose who they wished to bank with. That is, they could choose to bank through a variety of financial service providers, whether a mobile phone company, a post office or a bank.[30] However, the traditional route was trod, thanks to resistance from bankers and from within the Reserve Bank of India as well. The RBI thereafter announced that it would issue new kinds of licences and open up the process of setting up new banks. Notwithstanding the push, progress was slow to reach those who needed it most. As of 31 March 2014, the banking network comprised of 115,082 branches and 160,055 ATMs, of which barely a third of the branches served the 600,000-plus villages and only one-sixth of ATMs were in rural areas. And then there were 1.4 lakh business correspondents – who served as mobile banks serving customers of public sector and regional rural banks.

Enter the Jan Dhan Yojana. Speaking from the ramparts of the Red Fort on 15 August 2014, the PM announced, 'I have come here with a pledge to launch a scheme on this festival of Freedom. It will be called Pradhanmantri Jan Dhan Yojana (PMJDY). I wish to connect the poorest citizens of the country with the facility of bank accounts through this yojana. There are millions of families who have mobile phones but no bank accounts. We have to change this scenario. Economic resources of the country should be utilized for the well-being of the poor. The change will commence from this point.'[31] To propel the pull factor, new account holders would be given a Rupay debit card and an insurance cover of Rs 100,000.

The launch of PMJDY had the stamp of Modi the organiser. A signed letter from the prime minister was sent out by email to 725,000 bank officers across India through the government online system e-Sampark. Defining the magnitude of the task as 'gigantic' the prime minister said, 'We need to enrol over 7 crore households and open their accounts. This is a national priority and we must rise to meet this challenge. There is urgency to this exercise as all other development activities are hindered by this single disability. I am sure we will overcome this situation collectively.' A competition was held on the MyGov platform for suggesting a name, logo and tagline. Over 6,000 entries were received. Priya Sharma, an IP professional from Bengaluru, won the contest and a prize of Rs 25,000.[32] The tagline *Mera Khata Bhagya Vidhata* (My Account My Destiny Maker) was finalised.

On 28 August, PMJDY was launched simultaneously at state capitals, major cities and district headquarters. In all, seventy-six functions were planned across the country, to be attended by Union ministers, chief ministers and dignitaries. Public sector banks lined up 77,892 camps in rural and urban areas on the day. A documentary on financial inclusion and an exhibition on financial literacy and technology were part of the programme. Also on the agenda was the dedication of an UIDAI–National

Modification

Payments Corporation of India initiative for making available mobile banking facility on the basic phone using USSD (Unstructured Supplementary Service Data) technology. Twenty-six public sector banks and three private sector banks joined this platform.

The launch also had a target: to open 10 million accounts in one single day. Critical to this ambition was the use of Aadhaar-enabled KYC for opening new accounts. On 29 August, the government announced that 18,468,000 accounts had been opened. This success was to be followed up with weekly camps across India for PMJDY. Using a page from market players, the government also introduced incentives to boost enrolment – for instance, a life insurance cover for a nominal amount. This was valid for accounts opened before and up to Republic Day, 26 January 2015.

Aadhaar was not only back, but back on track.

•

On 10 September, the Cabinet Committee on Economic Affairs headed by the prime minister approved Phase V of the UIDAI programme and expansion in Uttar Pradesh, Bihar, Chhattisgarh and Uttarakhand – states with a high density of population. UIDAI, which by then had enrolled 673.8 million Aadhaar numbers at a cost of Rs 49.06 billion, was given funds and a target of 1,000 million, or one billion, by 2015.

The political play that accompanied the turnaround of Aadhaar is best illustrated by events and documentation thereof from Rajasthan. The government of Rajasthan, like many other state governments, had to file affidavits – through the local UIDAI office – in the ongoing matter in the Supreme Court. In December 2013, it said the Aadhaar scheme 'fosters and facilitates the various welfare schemes/subsidies to the intended beneficiary, provides easy identification for a person to avail government services; plugs leakages and pilferages in the system.' This was when there was a Congress government in Rajasthan and a Congress-led government at the Centre.

Subsequently, a supplementary was filed where the state illustrated the distinction between citizens and residents and stated, 'Poor verification of resident's credentials is cause of concern for the State Government.' It cited the right of states to deliver services, referred to its own Bhamashah programme and said the Aadhaar scheme was 'misconceived'. This was in February 2014 when there was a BJP government in the state and the Congress-led UPA at the Centre and elections had been announced. Following the launch of the Pradhanmantri Jan Dhan Yojana, the BJP government in Rajasthan performed an adroit side-step on paper.

As PMJDY picked up pace and acquired scale, the government got to work on the next phase of its plan. On 24 October, Dharmendra Pradhan, minister for petroleum, held a video conference to review the preparations for the launch of the modified Direct Benefit Transfer of LPG (DBTL) scheme in fifty-four districts on 15 November. It was the test run for expansion of DBTL.

UIDAI had completed enrolment of over 720 million Aadhaar numbers. Over 100 million bank accounts had been seeded with Aadhaar numbers, making them ready to receive benefits and transact on the NPCI platform for mobile banking. This included not just those on smart phones but also those using ordinary feature phones. The facility on feature phones allowed residents to check the status of the Aadhaar–bank account linkage by dialling *99*99# on their mobile phone.[33]

On 1 January 2015, the government launched PAHAL, its DBTL scheme, in 622 districts of the country.[34] Consumers could link their Aadhaar number to a bank account and the seventeen-digit LPG consumer number. They would pay the market price for the LPG cylinder and receive the subsidy directly in their bank account. The government announced that the scheme would cover over 153 million consumers across 676 districts of the country.

A week before the 25 January deadline for PMJDY accounts, referred to as Jan Dhan accounts, Finance Minister Jaitley announced that over 115 million bank accounts had been opened across the country. Prime Minister Modi wrote to bankers congratulating them on the success: 'By opening 11.5 crore (115 million) new accounts in a very short span, we have achieved a coverage of 99.74% of all households in the country. I congratulate you for your extraordinary efforts.' Between

August and December, global crude oil prices had fallen from US$104 to US$60 per barrel. Government spend on subsidies, though, was in excess of Rs 2.66 trillion. The government pushed on. By the end of January, over 97 million LPG consumers were covered under PAHAL. The government said it was now the largest cash transfer programme anywhere in the world.[35]

DBT's success seemed to inject testosterone shots into the idea of cash transfers. Its combined promise of savings and curbing of corruption, and captured the imagination of people and policy wonks. On 27 February 2015, the Economic Survey mooted the expansion of cash transfers to other welfare programmes. The survey said, 'The debate is not about whether but how best to provide active government support to the poor and vulnerable. Cash-based transfers based on the JAM number trinity – Jan Dhan, Aadhaar, Mobile – offer exciting possibilities to effectively target (deliver) public resources to those who need it most. Success in this area will allow prices to be liberated to perform their role of efficiently allocating resources and boosting long-run growth".'[36]

Aadhaar was, meanwhile, being taken to new sectors. The government was expanding its use for purposes such as digital lockers – a scheme under Digital India was launched to enable people to store their documents using Aadhaar numbers. Another area was Jeevan Pramaan, an online life certification system for pensioners, who otherwise had to physically present themselves before branch managers or seek letters from gazetted officers.

Modification

Other institutions too were keen to leverage Aadhaar. In March 2015, Chief Election Commissioner H.S. Brahma suggested authentication of electoral rolls via Aadhaar.

Jan Dhan Yojana entered the Guinness Records 'for most accounts opened in a week, that is, 18,096,130 accounts August 23 to 29, 2014.'[37] On the first anniversary of the Jan Dhan Yojana, the Finance Ministry revealed that 177.4 million accounts were opened, 42 per cent of them seeded with Aadhaar numbers, enabling transfer of over Rs 42.73 billion of MGNREGS wages and Rs 174.46 billion of subsidies under the DBT scheme.[38] Finance Minister Jaitley said, 'As a next step, the aim is to utilise these accounts for extending insurance, pension and credit facilities to those who are currently excluded from these benefits', to enable the poor 'in having a financial footprint' to improve their lot.

●

The ambitions of the UPA were reined in by both the absence of a law and of political order. The Modi government had established order from day one. But it was yet to address the issue of a statutory law and the legalities in several petitions pending before the Supreme Court.

On 22 July, the attorney general of India, Mukul Rohatgi, represented the government's view in court. Rohatgi was appointed as AG in June 2014 by the Modi government. Son of Justice Awadh Behari Rohatgi, a former Delhi High Court judge, Rohatgi had represented the Gujarat government in the Supreme Court in the 2002 Gujarat riots case. He had other high-profile cases and corporate clients to his name, and was known for his court craft and combative demeanour, with a booming voice and six-foot frame to go with it. Rohatgi challenged the view of petitioners who were concerned about violation of privacy, and asked the court to decide whether privacy was a fundamental right. He referred to earlier pronouncements of the Supreme Court, M.P. Sharma and others v Satish Chandra and others,[39] *AIR 1954 SC 300* and Kharak Singh v State of UP, *AIR 1963 SC 1295*,[40] decided by eight and six judges. Herein, Rohatgi maintained, the legal position regarding the existence of the fundamental right to privacy was doubtful. The AG also cited other judgements where the court had referred to the right to privacy.[41]

K.K. Venugopal, appearing for the Centre for Civil Society, and Rohatgi suggested that the matter be placed before a larger bench to look at, one, 'whether there is any "right to privacy" guaranteed under the Indian Constitution and, two, if such a right exists, what is its source and what are the contours of such a right, as there is no express provision in the Constitution adumbrating the right to privacy'. Gopal Subramanium and Shyam Divan, appearing for the petitioners, opposed 'the suggestion that this batch of matters is required to be heard by a larger bench'. Their point was: 'The conclusions recorded by this Court in R. Rajagopal[42] and PUCL[43] are legally tenable for the reason that the

Modification

observations made in M.P. Sharma regarding the absence of right to privacy under our Constitution are not part of ratio decidendi of that case and, therefore, do not bind the subsequent smaller Benches.'[44]

On 11 August 2015, the bench concluded that the matter be placed before the chief justice for appropriate orders. They also heard arguments on the legality of expansion of the Aadhaar Scheme on the basis of the order of 2013. The AG, saying that Aadhaar ensured effective implementation of welfare schemes like MGNREGA, the distribution of food, ration and kerosene through the PDS system and grant of subsidies in the distribution of LPG, told the court that the Union of India would ensure that Aadhaar cards would only be issued on a consensual basis.

The court then ordered the following:

1. The Union of India shall give wide publicity in the electronic and print media including radio and television networks that it is not mandatory for a citizen to obtain an Aadhaar card;
2. The production of an Aadhaar card will not be a condition for obtaining any benefits otherwise due to a citizen;
3. The Unique Identification Number or the Aadhaar card will not be used by the respondents for any purpose other than the PDS Scheme and in particular for the purpose of distribution of foodgrains, etc. and cooking fuel, such as

kerosene. The Aadhaar card may also be used for the purpose of the LPG Distribution Scheme;
4. The information about an individual obtained by the Unique Identification Authority of India while issuing an Aadhaar card shall not be used for any other purpose, save as above, except as may be directed by a Court for the purpose of criminal investigation.[45]

The order threw a ring of uncertainty around the use of Aadhaar for Jan Dhan and other schemes. The government then approached the Supreme Court for clarification. On 15 October 2015, the Supreme Court stated that the inclusion of National Social Assistance Programmes – Old Age Pensions, Widow Pensions, Disability Pensions, PMJDY and the Employees' Provident Fund Organisation – would not dilute the earlier order. It, however, impressed on the government 'to strictly follow all the earlier orders passed by this Court commencing from 23 September 2013 and to make it clear that the Aadhaar Card Scheme is purely voluntary and it cannot be made mandatory till the matter is finally decided by this Court one way or the other'.[46]

The government presented it as a victory, a validation of the use of Aadhaar. Critics saw the conditionality of 'purely voluntary' as a sign of hope for privacy. The concerns over data protection and privacy grew among the public and in Parliament. In the Lok Sabha, BJP MP Bhartendra Singh asked whether the government was aware of concerns being raised about privacy under the Digital India project and 'whether the government is taking steps to ensure privacy of information'. In the Rajya Sabha, trenchant and consistent critic Rajeev Chandrasekhar asked the minister of communications 'whether the government believes there is an urgent need to enact a privacy legislation to protect the rights of citizens vis-à-vis the various official databases of government which collates information about citizens'. Chandrasekhar followed this up with a letter to the prime minister, pointing out gaps in existing provisions and urging for a law on citizens' right to privacy.

On 4 November, Prime Minister Modi reviewed the progress of PMJDY and directed that awareness campaigns be launched, especially on mobile phones, about the benefits available through Jan Dhan accounts. He also asked all Chief Secretaries in various state governments to accelerate the adoption of Jan Dhan and Aadhaar to curb leakages, and so that benefits could reach the poor.[47] Two days later, at an economics conclave, Modi took on critics. 'What is the aim of reform? Is it just to increase the measured rate of GDP growth? Or is it to bring about a transformation in society? My answer is clear. We must reform to transform.'[48]

By November 2015, as per the government, 926 million Aadhaar numbers had been issued – of the twenty-four states UIDAI was enrolling in, sixteen states had reached 100 per cent adult saturation.[49]

The government was now dealing with a programme

that was already too big to falter, never mind fail. Executive action needed to be backed by legislation. Social security schemes and digital initiatives were now dependent on the legality of the use of the Aadhaar number and the cloud of uncertainty and concern needed to be dispelled. On 7 November 2015, Arun Jaitley announced that while the views of the government would be placed before the court, the draft legislation was ready. He declared, 'Aadhaar and the JAM trinity are here to stay.'[50] Meanwhile, speaking on the cashless economy at another forum, Nilekani observed, 'Ideally, the government should pass a law to back Aadhaar.'[51]

In December 2015, the Direct Benefit Transfer of LPG or PAHAL scheme entered the Guinness Book of World records as the largest cash transfer programme with over 146.2 million identified beneficiaries joining in.[52] Enthused, the government expanded the use of Aadhaar for the rollout of the National Food Security Act and asked states to follow the best practices of Jharkhand on digitisation and Aadhaar seeding. It was also encouraging the use of Aadhaar for micro, small and medium enterprises to improve ease of doing business besides leveraging Aadhaar-enabled payment systems to promote payments by card and by digital means to trim down use of cash in the economy. Aadhaar could be used as KYC for buying Sovereign Gold Bonds, for buying tickets for the Republic Day Parade and Beating Retreat.

On Republic Day, President Pranab Mukherjee said, 'Aadhaar, with its present reach of 96 crore people, is

Modification

helping in direct transfer of benefits, plugging leakages and improving transparency.' Aadhaar had come to be the punctuation in every conversation, conference and committee on governance.[53]

In January 2016, the World Bank's World Development Report endorsed the idea of Aadhaar and said, 'Technology can be transformational. A digital identification system such as India's Aadhaar, by overcoming complex information problems, helps willing governments to promote the inclusion of disadvantaged groups.'[54]

On 26 February, the Finance Ministry released Economic Survey 2015–16.[55] Chief Economic Adviser Arvind Subramaniam devoted seventeen pages in the survey on how the DBT was now used to deliver benefits worth Rs 440.35 billion to 296 million beneficiaries and outlining further possibilities. The survey asked a basic question: 'Suppose the government wanted to transfer Rs 1,000 to every Indian tomorrow. What would it require to do?' It answered, '1. Government must be able to identify beneficiaries; 2. Government must be able to transfer money to beneficiaries; 3. Beneficiaries must be able to easily access their money.' Finance Minister Jaitley presented the political message in Budget 2016. He said, 'we have embarked on game-changing reforms'. The JAM trinity, he said, would allow transfer of benefits in a leakage-proof, well-targeted and cashless manner.

The trinity required statutory cover. Jaitley introduced the Aadhaar (Targeted Delivery of Financial and Other

Subsidies, Benefits and Services) Bill 2016 in the Lok Sabha on 3 March. The preamble read, 'A Bill to provide for, as a good governance, efficient, transparent, and targeted delivery of subsidies, benefits and services, the expenditure for which is incurred from the Consolidated Fund of India, to individuals residing in India through assigning of unique identity numbers to such individuals and for matters connected therewith or incidental thereto.'

The BJP's Bill on Aadhaar had many changes that differentiated it from the Congress' Bill of 2010. In the UPA Bill, a resident was any person residing in India. The 2016 Bill defined the entity of resident as 'any person who has resided in India for 182 days'. It explicitly states that 'Aadhaar number shall not confer any right of citizenship or domicile to an Aadhaar number holder'. Clause 3(2) states, 'The enrolling agency shall, at the time of enrolment, inform the individual undergoing enrolment of the following details in such manner as may be specified by regulations, namely: (a) the manner in which the information shall be used; (b) with whom the information is intended to be shared during authentication; (c) the existence of a right to access information, the procedure for making requests for access, and details of the person or department in-charge to whom such requests can be made.' Also stated were restrictions on sharing of information under Clause 8 (4); Clause 29(1), (4), and also on protection of the data.[56]

Modification

The strategy in the phrasing of the preamble, 'expenditure for which is incurred from the Consolidated Fund of India' was two-pronged. It enabled the government to expand the use of Aadhaar in virtually every government programme and project. It also, critically, gave the government the language to introduce it as a Money Bill. The Modi government had done its ground work. The BJP had a majority in the Lok Sabha but fell short of it in the Rajya Sabha. Following the debacle on the amendment to the land acquisition act, the government knew it would be blockaded in the Rajya Sabha. A Money Bill deals with the expenditure of government and does not require the clearance of the Rajya Sabha.

Naturally there was uproar across the Opposition benches. Congress's Mallikarjun Kharge, Leader of the Opposition in the Lok Sabha, said: 'We are ready to cooperate on the Bill but it should not come as a Money Bill. They are doing this to avoid Rajya Sabha ... You have made your intention clear.' Jaitley said it was for the speaker, Sumitra Mahajan, to take the final call on whether or not it could be classified as a Money Bill. He cited Section 110 of the Constitution in defence of the government – the said section defines in seven clauses any bill which dealt with payment of, or withdrawal of, money from the Consolidated Fund of India as a Money Bill.[57]

Due to the outrage – justifiable, on the modus of legislation – what did not receive adequate attention from the lawmakers in Parliament, and therefore the public, was the minutiae of the proposed law. On 11 March, the Lok Sabha passed Aadhaar Act 2016.[58]

The Opposition made itself heard on their and the public's fear about loss of privacy, about individual and mass surveillance. Tathagata Satpathy of Biju Janata Dal said the project could be used for mass surveillance or ethnic cleansing in the future. Asaduddin Owaisi of the AIMIM and Kaushalendra Kumar of the JD (U) echoed similar concerns. Bhartruhari Mahtab of BJD said the Bill should not be rushed, it should be sent for consideration to a parliamentary panel. In response, the government pointed to provisions that promised protection of data and its use. Jaitley referred to the 'consent' in Clause 3(2) and added, 'The purpose of the bill is not for collateral purpose' but to reach welfare to beneficiaries.

During discussion on the Bill in the Rajya Sabha, Sitaram Yechury of CPM, Naresh Agrawal of SP and K.C. Tyagi from JD (U) protested the Money Bill classification. The Congress's Jairam Ramesh described it as knocking 'a nail in the coffin of the Upper House'. On 16 March, the Opposition recommended several amendments including on the use of Aadhaar. Jairam Ramesh suggested restricting the use of Aadhaar only for government benefits, to allow alternate and viable means of identification, a provision to opt out, and for changing the term 'national security' to 'public emergency' or 'public safety'.[59] The irony that those who propounded the idea and expansion of Aadhaar were now arguing

Modification

for an 'alternate' was lost in the din. These were voted seventy-seven for and sixty-four against. The Lok Sabha rejected all the amendments and passed the Bill as it had passed it the first time on March 11.

On 4 April 2016, UIDAI crossed the ten-digit mark – it had registered one billion or 100 crore Aadhaar numbers.

The government announced that 93 per cent of the adults in the country now had an Aadhaar number. It claimed that with nearly half a million enrolments every day, Aadhaar was the largest online digital identity platform in the world. It enabled over 84 million eKYC transactions and over 1.5 billion authentications. UIDAI was directed to push special enrolment drives in states where enrolment was slow and low.

On 7 April, Jairam Ramesh filed a petition (*WP(C) 231/2016*) in the Supreme Court challenging the introduction and passing of the Aadhaar Act as a Money Bill. On 25 April, P. Chidambaram, appearing for Ramesh, sought issuance of notice on the plea. A bench led by Chief Justice T.S. Thakur said they would like to have the views of the attorney general. On 10 May 2016, the attorney general argued that the decision of the speaker of the Lok Sabha to treat a Bill as a Money Bill was not open for judicial review. Rohatgi also said that there was no violation of any fundamental right of the Congress leader and hence a writ petition under Article 32 was not maintainable.[60] The court then asked the petitioners to submit a note of their submissions and case laws.

In the meantime, the government went ahead with the processes of law. Between July and September 2016, rules and guidelines were notified for the Aadhaar Act. In October, a fresh petition was filed in the Supreme Court by S.G. Vombatkere v Union of India, *WP(C) 797/2016*. It challenged the Aadhaar Act as also the rules and regulations notified therein.

Aadhaar was making news elsewhere too. On 6 October 2016, the World Bank held a conference titled 'Identification for Development: Harnessing the Power of Digital Solutions'. Naturally, Aadhaar occupied centre stage in the discussions. Paul Romer, chief economist at the World Bank tweeted, 'Nandan, you've launched something extraordinary. Took 30 years before GPS had first commercial app. I bet Aadhaar will kick in much faster.'[61] 'The system in India is the most sophisticated that I've seen,' Romer said subsequently. 'It's the basis for all kinds of connections that involve things like financial transactions. It could be good for the world if this became widely adopted.'[62]

The United Nations in its report on sustainable development goals titled 'Leave No One Behind' said, 'The decision of India in 2010 to launch the Aadhaar programme to enrol the biometric identifying data of all its 1.2 billion citizens, for example, was a critical step in enabling fairer access of the people to government benefits and services.'[63]

●

Modification

On the evening of 8 November 2016, Indians turned on their television sets and found Prime Minister Modi on all the news channels. In a move that stunned an unsuspecting nation into silence, he announced the demonetisation of all 500-rupee and 1,000-rupee notes from midnight. He declared that 'five hundred and thousand rupee notes hoarded by anti-national and anti-social elements will become just worthless pieces of paper'. He went on to say that 'the rights and the interests of honest, hard-working people will be fully protected' and that the demonetisation would 'strengthen the hands of the common man in the fight against corruption, black money and fake currency'.

The move triggered chaos and systemic failures ensued. A large part of India's economy is informal and runs on cash. The human cost was stark and visible. The queues at ATMs, the loss of earnings for daily wage earners, the loss of business for small businesses, the misery of farmers selling daily produce and the reported death of over eighty persons saw Opposition parties up in arms against the move and the government.

There had been two demonetisations before – in 1946 and 1978. The difference this time was the brutal magnitude. The Modi government had sucked out over Rs 15.4 trillion of a total of Rs 16.9 trillion of currency in circulation: roughly 87 per cent of all cash in the system. Demonetisation was severely criticised by economists and politicians. Former Prime Minister Manmohan Singh, in a rare intervention in Parliament, described it as 'organised loot and legalised plunder' and predicted that demonetisation could hurt GDP growth by nearly 2 per cent.

NaMo's Demo, as it was dubbed, became the trending topic for weeks thereafter in newspapers, and prime-time television swung between stories pitching potential benefits versus some sort of contest of hardships. Staying away from such binaries, living room and political conversations theorised that this was to gain advantage in the forthcoming polls in Uttar Pradesh. The queues at the ATMs continued for weeks, pictures and reports of empty ATMs occupied front-page space. Even though every currency press was operating on full capacity and all shifts, they struggled to meet the huge gap – they also produced collector's items in misprints. The debate was how long the crisis would last.

Modi used the crisis as an opportunity to push the country towards a less-cash economy with digital payments. The Aadhaar platform made this possible. In December 2016, India had over a billion persons registered under Aadhaar. The country had over a billion mobile subscriptions – of whom nearly 800 million were estimated to be unique users. India also had a financial transaction architecture ready in the Unified Payments Interface, an interoperable mobile-first payment system, a uniquely Indian achievement led by the National Payments Corporation of India.

The government brought all the three pieces – Aadhaar registrations, mobile users and network, and payment gateways into play. On 30 November, NITI Aayog constituted a committee of chief ministers representing different political parties to examine and promote the use of digital payment systems across the country. The government also announced a slew of incentives to encourage people to move from cash to a digital platform. To reduce transaction costs of digital payments fees, charges levied by banks and on government portals were reduced or done away with.

On 30 December, Modi launched BHIM, drawing on the name of a key framer of the Constitution and Dalit icon Dr Bhimrao Ramji Ambedkar, an app for digital transactions that was operable first on smart phones and later on feature phones. He appealed to the public to undertake at least five transactions daily through mobile phones and let the country lead the digital movement.

By 1 January, BHIM was the top download from Google Playstore. The government pushed digital payments by having Niti Aayog and other departments conduct what was described as Digi Dhan Melas. For ninety days, a rewards scheme was deployed – over 1.4 million consumers and 77,000 merchants participated. The volume of various digital transactions (including online, apps and USSD) increased about twenty-three-fold with 6,380,000 digital transactions for a value of Rs 24.25 billion in March 2017 compared to 280,000 digital transactions worth Rs 1.01 billion in November 2016. Over 700,000 merchants and twenty-seven banks were on the BHIM platform.[64]

The debate has since shifted, to whether this trend would be lasting and lead to digitisation of payments or peter out as more cash became available in the economy. The jury is out.

On 22 March, the government inducted a new element in the use of Aadhaar that triggered controversy and new fears about possibilities of surveillance and loss of privacy. As part of the Finance Bill, an amendment to the Income Tax Act 1961 was passed, making Aadhaar mandatory for filing tax returns. The amendment introduced in Section 139AA also made Aadhaar mandatory for applying for PAN cards starting 1 July 2017. The move was backed by a recommendation of the SIT on Black Money which said people have the option of 'quoting their PAN or UID or Passport number or any proof of identity. However there is no mechanism/system to connect the data available with each' and suggested that the databases be interconnected.[65]

On 26 April, the Supreme Court heard a new PIL, Binoy Viswam v Union of India, *WP(C) 247/2017*, on the mandatory linking of Aadhaar with PAN along with S.G. Vombatkere and another vs Union of India. Mukul Rohatgi, attorney general of India, told the Supreme Court that while 290 PAN cards had been issued, only 50 million were assessees. He advocated linking Aadhaar to PAN card and income tax returns was critical to weed out fakes and duplicates.[66]

The matter on linking Aadhaar to PAN card was heard by the Supreme Court on 4 May 2017 and orders

Modification

were reserved. On 31 May 2017, the Income Tax Department, via the media and SMS messages, urged tax payers to link PAN card number with the Aadhaar number.

On 9 June, the Supreme Court bench of Justice A.K. Sikri and Ashok Bhushan upheld the validity of Section 139AA and the government's move to make the quoting of Aadhaar number mandatory while filing tax returns for all those who had one. The Court observed that 'Parliament was fully competent to enact Section 139AA of the Act and its authority to make this law was not diluted by the orders of this Court.' The PAN card remains valid for now.

On 10 June, the Income Tax Department issued a reminder that those applying for PAN cards must submit their Aadhaar numbers.

While the issue of privacy as a right is yet to be settled, between August 2015, when the Supreme Court referred the issue of privacy to a Constitution Bench, and May 2017, the government has passed the Aadhaar Act 2016, issued multiple notifications and expanded the scope of Aadhaar usage.

Aadhaar is deployed for identity, for verification of electoral rolls, for issue of a Universal Account Number for Provident Fund account holders, in digital payments, for Direct Benefit Transfers, for PM Ujwala Yojana, for old-age pension schemes, for rural housing schemes, for the rural employment guarantee programme, for scholarships, for government fellowships, for issue of passport, for registration of vehicles, for issue of licences, and more. Between January and March 2017, there were over fifty government gazetted notifications linking nearly 100 welfare programmes of the Centre and the states to Aadhaar.

Aadhaar has come to be the motherboard of connectivity. Satya Nadella, CEO of Microsoft, describes the Aadhaar platform as an 'hour glass' architecture. What this means is that the basic identity system is, and can be, host to numerous applications above the stem. It is inspired by what the US did with internet, GPS and other public-funded research that created platforms for civil society to build applications on. The Modi government has leveraged every application and added many more.

In June 2017, Aadhaar reached a new milestone: 1,150,000,000 enrolments.

UIDAI has statutory status. However, the idea of unique identity – the aadhaar of each individual – awaits the legitimacy of a law. A law on privacy that will help preserve the uniqueness of personhood.

Epilogue
RIGHT TO PRIVACY AND GETTING IT RIGHT

'As every man goes through life he fills in a number of forms for the record, each containing a number of questions. A man's answer to one question on one form becomes a little thread, permanently connecting him to the local centre of personnel records administration. There are thus hundreds of little threads radiating from every man, millions of threads in all. If these threads were suddenly to become visible, the whole sky would look like a spider's web, and if they materialised as elastic bands, buses, trams and even people would all lose the ability to move, and the wind would be unable to carry torn newspapers or autumn leaves along the streets of the city. They are not visible, they are not material, but every man is constantly aware of their existence ... Each man, permanently aware of his own invisible threads, naturally develops a respect for the people who manipulate the threads ...'

—Alexander Solzhenitsyn,
Cancer Ward, 1966

Epilogue

Solzhenitsyn on the surveillance state, on the realities of that numbing chill a paternalistic state can perpetrate on its residents, reverberates in every discourse on data protection and privacy, particularly in India half a century later. With more than 1,150 million Aadhaar numbers issued, with the government rapidly augmenting Aadhaar as the prime connector between itself and the number holder, there is a sense of disquiet about 'Big Brother', about being put on an electronic leash by the state, around data leaks and on identity theft.

The fears are not irrational. They are echoes of expressions in the approach paper to privacy, put out by the Government of India in 2010: 'One of the inevitable consequences of the UID project will be that the UID number will unify multiple databases. As more and more agencies of the government sign on to the UID project, the UID number will become the common thread that links all those databases together.'[1] Shades of Solzhenitsyn.

That there is a gap in the law for 'security and protection of personal data collected by various government and private agencies' and that this if-and-when seamlessly interconnected 'will make it rather difficult for an individual to go about the business of daily life'[2] was underlined in the briefing note for an Inter-ministerial Committee of Secretaries set up to look at the legal landscape for data protection.

The 'growth of e-commerce, e-governance, projects of the government, creation of databases and greater usage

Epilogue

of IT both by government and body corporates, and consequently decision-making on automated systems, cautioned the note, 'call for a sound legal framework to protect the data with uniform standards applicable to all. The concerns for data protection arise from possible data loss, unauthorised access and misuse of data, fraud, loss of reputation, financial loss, promotional marketing and cross-selling, compromised data through wrongful exclusion and denial of services and undesirable uses such as profiling, tracking and violation of rights.' The reality is that the Information Technology Act 2000, as amended in 2008, covers data protection across private entities but not governmental bodies. And where there are justiciable provisions – in banking, for instance – they are limited to the domain.

Vexing the issue of absence is the presence of a legal conflict between transparency and protection. The RTI Act requires departments to publish details of execution of programmes. The approach paper for the proposed legislation on privacy pointed out that while transparency was a good thing, the issue was one of unintended consequences. 'With the introduction of the UID number this practice could result in even greater harm as the UID number that will be present in each and every publication of this nature will make it easy to link various public databases and help create an identifiable profile of everyone on that public database.'

The essence of the many articulations is that either by a systemic flaw or by an executive fiat, that is, by

Epilogue

accident or by design, personal data could be outed, as it was possible to connect the various databases to create identifiable profiles and this could result in tracking or targeting of individuals and violation of rights.

In 2010, Britain abandoned the biometrics-enabled national ID project after much debate. The nub was the lack of a 'foundation of public trust and confidence'. It's true that the objectives and the context of the abandoned British project – the complexities as also the scale, their comparatively very low population – are very different from those of Aadhaar. But what does stand out in mid-2017 is the need to instil public trust and confidence.

Fear triggers anxiety; fuelling such anxieties have been the political and personal proxy wars, within government and outside it. The suspicions stem from many silos – systemic issues, inadequacy of capacity in government, legal infirmities, toleration of apathy, failure of mechanisms for redressal and, above all, the absence of a law for data protection and privacy. The conflation of issues – the general with the particular – is leading to all the systemic failures being personified in Aadhaar. It is important to look at these issues in granular detail. The endeavour in the following pages is to examine the cases and complaints and look at possible solutions.

What can be done to prevent leakage of personal identifiable information, curb failures of biometric authentication and prevent exclusion of the poor? Why is it important to create real-time grievance redressal mechanisms? Are Aadhaar numbers being duplicated or are cards being forged, and what can be done about it? How must government prevent identity theft? What could be the arrangement to give individuals control over their data? What is the precept of privacy and what could be the template conditions for a law that guarantees personhood?

These concerns, possible approaches and solutions are laid out in separate sections below.

Systemic Fault Lines

The issues dogging Aadhaar were highlighted by two incidents. A postman in Dantaramgarh, in Sikar in Rajasthan, was baffled at being expected to deliver a card for the Hindu deity Lord Hanuman, son of Pawan, with Aadhaar number 2094705195411.[3] In Kanjasa, near Allahabad, over a thousand villagers found they had the same birth date, 1 January, when they received their Aadhaar cards.[4] The government clarified in Parliament that action had been taken – over 34,000 operators had been blacklisted for 'polluting' the UIDAI eco-system, 1,000 between December 2016 and April 2017. That 1,000 operators needed to be barred in a five-month period was evidence of deep flaws.[5] There were also instances of 'websites and mobile applications providing unauthorised Aadhaar-related services such as downloading online Aadhaar letters, providing status of Aadhaar generation, printing Aadhaar letters on Polyvinyl chloride (PVC) card etc.' raised in Parliament by Jyotiraditya Scindia and Gaurav Gogoi.[6]

Epilogue

The government admitted as much in the Lok Sabha and informed the house that the illegal websites were subsequently blocked by the Department of Telecom and apps taken off Google Playstore. Blacklisting and blocking are necessary measures but not sufficient. The violation of rules and attempts to exploit the system demand tighter scrutiny of who is allowed to enrol and exemplary punishment for violators to deter repetition.

The bigger issue driving angst and activism is exclusion. Aadhaar is meant to be an enabler of inclusion to ensure the poor, in villages and in urban areas, are not denied access to public services. There is a gap between promise and performance. When a beneficiary at a fair-price or ration shop authenticates that s/he is a valid claimant to receive food-grain quota, he/she is confronted by the ineptness of personnel coupled with the insufficiency of infrastructure. State sloth only serves to compound it. Pre-Aadhaar, claimants for food-grain quotas were dealing with known variables – the vagaries of supplies to ration shops, the whims of the shop owners and dealers in making it available to them. Post Aadhaar, they have to deal with additional variables – fingerprint registrations and data connectivity.

Nikhil Dey, an activist with the Mazdoor Kisan Shakti Sangathan, spells it out. 'When I go to the ration shop, I am required to give my thumb impression. It often happens that either the Internet is not working or the machine is malfunctioning. Everyone in the village, including the shop owner, knows I am Nikhil. But my

Epilogue

rights are detained, or I am deprived because the machine does not certify that I am Nikhil. I am excluded.' Dey says the system needs to deliver to at least 98 per cent efficacy whereas in many areas it identifies only 30 or 40 per cent and many are denied their due. He adds, 'Even those who pass the authentication process are being denied entitlements at ration/PDS shops despite availability of stocks.' Entrenched corruption is clearly circumventing the Aadhaar gateway – the shop owner continues to hold sway. Such reports are coming from different rural areas of India as also cities.

The issue of exclusion found expression in Parliament. On 10 April 2017, Congress MP Jairam Ramesh told the house that, in Andhra Pradesh, where biometrics was being made compulsory for food-grain distribution, 'there are fifty types of errors by which you can deprive a ration card holder of his or her entitlement'. He said the same was true for old-age pension and charged that the Rajasthan government had deleted 10 lakh out of 54 lakh pensioners from the list. In a signed article Nikhil Dey and Magsaysay Award winner Aruna Roy say 'they were classified as "dead", "duplicates", or simply "other reasons".' Roy and Dey accessed the list to find eight of twelve persons in Rajasmand district classified as dead were alive. But their pensions had been stopped. 'One thousand, three hundred and ten persons out of the 2,900 classified as "dead" or "duplicates" in Bhim Block were found to be alive.'

At the core is the state of preparedness of the

government agencies to put Aadhaar to work. V. Vijai Sai Reddy of the YSR Congress, pointed out in the Rajya Sabha, 'Aadhaar-based biometric authentication in PDS outlets suffers from infrastructural bottlenecks', including lack of internet connectivity.

The push for pull factor worked to boost demand and enrolments but it was not matched by a push on the supply side by creating necessary infrastructure. The Economic Survey of 2015–16, while evangelising the idea of the Jan Dhan Aadhaar Mobile trinity, stated that 'The average state preparedness is 12 per cent' and pointed to states like Andhra Pradesh (96 per cent), Chhattisgarh (42 per cent) and Madhya Pradesh (27 per cent) which did better. It also said that 'the banking system remains limited, and BCs and mobile money providers have not yet solved this last-mile problem'.[7]

Grave authentication failures continued to occur, by the government's own admission. The Economic Survey of 2016–17 states, 'While Aadhaar coverage speed has been exemplary, with over a billion Aadhaar cards being distributed, some states report authentication failures: estimates include 49 percent failure rates for Jharkhand, 6 percent for Gujarat, 5 percent for Krishna District in Andhra Pradesh and 37 percent for Rajasthan. Failure to identify genuine beneficiaries results in exclusion errors.'[8]

The bungled introduction of Aadhaar for the Midday Meals Scheme is a case in point. This programme, which provides for free lunches in government schools to encourage the poor to send their children to school,

Epilogue

was first introduced in Tamil Nadu in 1982. While it has encouraged enrolments and consequently enabled improved literacy, the food provided to the children is often sub-standard, thanks to bureaucratic sloth and corruption. The government's case for introducing Aadhaar is that contractors pad up the number of students to mint money. Fact is, all schools, and the education department of the state government, are expected to have ready data on the number of students. Instead of fixing this very real problem in a methodical manner – by making the officials accountable – Aadhaar was used as a whip to crop out 'ghost entries' in the lists of students. Surely responsibility should have first been fixed at an administrative level and the Aadhaar registration aligned to the academic year instead of targeting children. It is critical that we do not exacerbate systemic issues which end up punishing the innocent.

The stark reality is the wide chasm between availability of provisions in laws and enforcement. For instance, when ration shop owners deny beneficiaries it is a violation of the justiciable Right to Food Act. The nexus that nurtures fraud in mid-day meals is covered by multiple provisions of CrPC, IPC and the anti-corruption laws.

The road ahead requires governments to understand that Aadhaar cannot be a cure-all potion for all the ills that afflict governance. The responsibility for ensuring capacity and capability, and enforcing accountability falls squarely on Central and state governments.

Fact is, these last-mile failures of governance are visiting Aadhaar. Can such systemic sloth short-circuit Aadhaar? To prevent this, the government must hasten to fix supply side issues – expand access to banking, accelerate the fibre-optics project to improve connectivity. To preclude exclusion, it may be worthwhile to consider multi-modal biometrics like finger-vein or palm-vein matching, expand authentication factors – fingerprint plus iris and SMS. Above all, government needs to assess the state of preparedness every time Aadhaar is deployed.

Fakes, Forgeries and Frauds

Periodically, the Aadhaar enrolment process is held hostage to regional and sub-national politics – this is visible in the halting of card-issuance and expansion in states like Assam and Jammu and Kashmir. Enrolment is 7 per cent in Assam, 9 per cent in Meghalaya.[9] Clearly there is a need for policy innovation to enable inclusion without compromising on national security objectives.

Members of Parliament, like BJP MP from Maharashtra, Kirit Somaiya, and several others from Assam, and elsewhere, have in the past expressed their anger over illegal immigrants – expressly Bangladeshis – showing up on the voters list. In this context Aadhaar has become the bugbear of many, not just politicians. Conversations in middle-class living rooms are peppered with comments about Nepalis – who form a large chunk of circular labour migration in India – Bangladeshis and Pakistanis acquiring Aadhaar cards. It is a committed belief among many that Aadhaar numbers have been issued without any supporting documents.

Earlier chapters have traced how Aadhaar went from being a unique identity number to a card, how the address was meant to be a communication address only, how successive governments decided to enable it as point of proof-of-identity and proof-of-address, so much so that today it is valid for a range of documents and mandatory for others. In the issuing of passports, for instance, it is stated that 'Furnishing of Aadhaar card will expedite processing of passport applications'.

In April 2017, Rajeev Chandrashekhar, Rajya Sabha MP, claimed in Parliament that forgery was common and fake Aadhaar cards were being printed for Rs 40 and that 'Aadhaar Numbers are available for Rs 2 per entry. I can give as many as the Minister wants.' Referring to 'two Pakistani spies being caught with Aadhaar cards made out in fake names, but with their biometrics' he asked, if there is a terror attack, 'whom should we sue?'[10] In May 2017, four Pakistani citizens in Bengaluru were found to be in possession of Aadhaar cards which they had procured for Rs 300, so as to get ration cards and other documents.[11]

The Bengaluru incidents exposed the influence of cash 'n carry, or the daily corruption at local levels of government. The concern was about national security, and also about routine breaking of rules. The issue came back to systemic debilities, due process and diligence.

Fakes, duplicates and forgeries have dogged Indian

Epilogue

systems. In February 2015, H.S. Brahma, then Chief Election Commissioner, stated that 85 million names on India's electoral rolls were fake or duplicate.[12] In April 2016, the government revealed in Parliament that the Income Tax Department had cancelled 1.15 million duplicate PAN cards. In June 2016, Finance Secretary Ashok Lavasa told media persons that the government had weeded out 160 million duplicate and bogus ration cards.[13] Road Transport Minister Nitin Gadkari told reporters in May 2016 that 30 per cent of driving licences were bogus and his officials added that the ministry had collated data and found that of the about 180 million drivers' licences, an estimated 54 million fell under the 'bogus' category.[14]

Their solution to stop fakes and duplicates? Link ration cards, driving licences, PAN cards to Aadhaar numbers. Brahma mooted linking Aadhaar to voter ID cards to purge the rolls of duplicates and fakes. Gadkari favours linking driving licences to Aadhaar. The Department of Telecom has asked mobile operators to use Aadhaar to verify subscriber identity. While introducing amendments to the Finance Bill, 2017, Finance Minister Arun Jaitley defended section 139AA of the Income Tax Act and linking of PAN cards with Aadhaar saying, 'In a situation where it has come to light that one citizen has up to five PAN cards, to avoid that, we have linked the PAN to Aadhaar.'

The expansion has compounded fears. Can the Aadhaar number be forged? At the time of going to press,

Epilogue

no one person has claimed to have, or has been found to have, two Aadhaar numbers. It may be surmised that the process of biometric registration and authentication of ten fingers and the iris scan precludes this. What is being forged or 'created' is the Aadhaar card. It is possible, as has been claimed, to use a number belonging to someone else and forge a card with the other demographic details. Not unsurprising in a country where new currency notes of Rs 2,000 were found forged within days of its issue, post the November 2016 demonetisation.

A point that needs to be raised here is whether the Aadhaar number dies with the death of the person. And, if so, how would the relevant communication reach UIDAI so that it can kill the number? The matter is vital because there are nearly 9 million deaths every year, and many of these individuals would be beneficiaries of entitlements.

These fissures in the system must be fixed. To start with this calls for clear communication by governments that possession of the card itself does not create entitlement rights. Usage must be made subject to biometric authentication – be it for foodgrains, opening a new bank account or a new mobile connection. Expansion of eKYC, e-authentication and two- or three-factor authentication could help render faking of cards unfruitful. The introduction of security features on the card, like on currency notes, could also be considered to make it less easy for photocopy forgers. And yes, the most doable part of this drive would be for governments to clamp down on the parallel economy for ration cards, driving licences and PAN cards. Caution begins at home.

Identity Theft

Lost and forgotten passwords can always be changed. If your signature is forged, you can always change it. What happens if your fingerprints are stolen? You cannot change those. What happens when your iris scan is stolen? It cannot be replaced.

Identity theft is no longer a fantastic idea scripted for the movies. Biometric theft does not require scooping out someone's eyeballs to get an IRIS scan or a thumb cut off for fingerprints as depicted in the thrillers – lifeless biometrics don't work anyway.

In December 2014, at a cybersecurity convention in Hamburg, a hacker known as Starbug, from the Chaos Computer Club, a hacker collective formed in Berlin in 1981, cloned the thumbprint of German Defence Minister Ursula von der Leyen after photographing her hand.[15] Starbug's objective was to question the credibility of fingerprint security systems. In 2015, researchers at Carnegie Mellon University in the US showed how they could identify drivers using iris scan technology from images of their eye captured from the vehicle's side mirror, from a distance of 40 feet.[16] These can be viewed as a reflection of possibilities for the improvement of security and to identify violators. They can also be viewed as proof of the vulnerabilities of biometrics.

As for hacking, it's a nightmare that seems to be

Epilogue

here to stay. In December 2015, a hacker uncovered a database on the web comprising various pieces of personal information related to 191 million American citizens registered to vote.[17] In December 2016, Russian hackers got into the Pentagon and seized the email system used by the Joint Chiefs of Staff and 3,500 military officers and civilians.[18] The Pentagon had to take the network down and replace the software and hardware. In March 2017, personal details of 33 million US employees, including military personnel, collated and available with a private company were released online.[19] Russian hackers also got into the website of the Democratic Party in the US.

Just as governments and companies worry about cyber security, a section of Aadhaar number holders is worried about the security of their biometric data vested with UIDAI. More so since these are increasingly getting linked with other multiple aspects of their lives: financial, social, property-holding, et al.

The biometric and demographic data of over one billion Indians are in the vaults of the Central Identities Data Repository. There are two issues at play here – the security of the core biometric and demographic data in CIDR and the security of data with the government, with various departments, which is characterised as personal identifiable information. In April and May 2017, a series of reports – including the headline catcher outing of the Aadhaar details of Indian cricket star M.S. Dhoni – deepened the sense of unease about the vulnerability

Epilogue

of personal data. Two researchers from the Centre for Internet and Society trawled the net and found from just four government websites data of over 130 million Aadhaar card holders leaked into the public domain.[20] The revelation – 9,432,605 bank accounts and 1,498,919 post office accounts linked with Aadhaar numbers out in public – was horrifying. The small consolation was that while the leaked numbers could be used by forgers, the Aadhaar number by itself could not be deployed without authentication.

Put on the defensive, the government claimed the data was safe while Opposition politicians held that the breach 'makes a mockery of all that Jaitley and Ravi Shankar Prasad have said in Parliament'.[21] Congress Vice-president Rahul Gandhi injected reason amidst the outrage to say, 'I am proud that we took the lead on Aadhaar, but let us not compromise a great initiative by turning a blind eye to major privacy and security concerns.'[22]

The question to be addressed here is what was 'leaked' and who leaked it. At work was the classic left-hand right-hand syndrome of government. Section 29(4) of the Aadhaar Act 2016 states, 'No Aadhaar number or core biometric information collected or created under this Act in respect of an Aadhaar number holder shall be published, displayed or posted publicly, except for the purposes as may be specified by regulations.' On the other hand, departments executing welfare programmes are obliged under Section 4-b (xii) of the RTI Act to

Epilogue

publish 'the manner of execution of subsidy programmes, including the amounts allocated and the details of beneficiaries of such programmes'.[23]

In May 2017, the attorney general admitted to the Supreme Court that there was leakage, or disclosure as the government put it, but it was not from UIDAI. Ram Sewak Sharma, former UIDAI chief and now Chairman of TRAI, comes up with a middle path: 'Mask the numbers except for the last four digits' as done by credit card companies and banks. The advice has been well received. Officials in ministries are being sensitised about the consequences of data breach and ministries are being asked to encrypt the Aadhaar number and personal financial details.[24]

How safe is the biometric data? How safe is CIDR from hacking? Both the UPA and now the NDA governments have consistently maintained that data in the CIDR vaults is safe. Nandan Nilekani asserts there is no question of the data being hacked. 'Show me even one instance of data theft. Aadhaar is very, very secure,' he says confidently. This confidence stems from the technical aspects of encryption. The biometric data, UIDAI claims on its website, is encrypted using the 'highest available public key cryptography encryption (PKI-2048 and AES-256) with each data record having a built-in mechanism to detect any tampering'.[25]

And how good is that? Bruce Schneier, author of *Data and Goliath: The Hidden Battles to Collect Your Data and Control Your World* and fellow at the

Berkman Center for Internet & Society at Harvard Law School and an expert on computer security and cryptography says, 'The algorithms are fine. They are excellent choices.' Cryptography algorithms, he adds, 'are, by far, the strongest link in any security chain'. He cautions that an attack against a system is more likely to exploit vulnerable areas – in the software, or the implementation, or the underlying computer or user interface. In short, one can never be too sure given the speed at which technology is evolving – particularly in computing power and in artificial intelligence. Threat perceptions are fluid. In 2016, the US National Security Agency shifted to, and recommended, a higher level of encryption (RSA 3072 with AES 256).[26] Eternal vigilance is the price for digital convenience, just as it is with democracy.

The question which people want an answer for is: who does one go to if personal identifiable information is leaked, if biometrics is compromised? In a signed article titled 'The Aadhaar We Deserve', Rajeev Chandrashekhar points out, 'Unfortunately the Aadhaar Act and accompanying regulations place no accountability on UIDAI to protect the database of citizens' personal information and are silent on the liability of the UIDAI and its personnel in case of non-compliance.'[27]

Vrinda Bhandari, an advocate and Renuka Sane, a researcher at the Indian Statistical Institute, found in their analysis 'Is Aadhaar grounded in adequate law and regulations?' that while notifying the regulations,

Epilogue

multiple aspects were left to be 'specified by authority'. 'Through the four substantive regulations, the phrase specified by the Authority has been used 51 times.'[28]

The fog on accountability must be cleared. Section 47 of the Aadhaar Act 2016 says, 'No court shall take cognisance of any offence punishable under this Act, save on a complaint made by the Authority or any officer or person authorised by it.'[29] Does this mean the individual has no power even to initiate proceedings and has to depend on the Authority to initiate criminal proceedings? Is the provision to file a regular FIR under IPC enough?

The road ahead must be cleared by recognising the right of the sovereign, the people, to seek redressal. Justice cannot be hostage to systemic flaws and apathy. Perhaps Section 47 was framed as a transitory measure as UIDAI transitioned from executive to statutory status. It is necessary for government to review this provision and restore the right to seek justice. The law must specify who is to be accountable, where the buck stops. Furthermore, data leakage and identity theft must fall under real-time disclosure and a mechanism for a speedy redressal system and options for compensation must be enshrined in law. And what if biometrics is indeed stolen? Life cannot grind to a halt. There is a need to work on Plan B – either an option to opt out or an alternate mechanism.

The Right to Privacy

The primary question that arises in the digital trail of Aadhaar is that of the right to privacy. There clearly is a need for a law in India that safeguards the privacy of individuals. Apart from the discourse about the Orwellian state – those who lived through the Emergency years know a bit about that – there is also a sense of vulnerability as individuals are drawn, even pushed, into the connected world, into digitisation.

The preamble of the Aadhaar Act of 2016 describes it as 'An act to provide for, as a good governance, efficient, transparent, and targeted delivery of subsidies, benefits and services, the expenditure for which is incurred from the Consolidated Fund of India, to individuals residing in India through assigning of unique identity numbers to such individuals and for matters connected therewith or incidental thereto.' Arguably any activity of the government paid for from the Consolidated Fund of India – ranging from supply of subsidised grains and LPG, to use of roads and civic amenities, and even, at a stretch, rebates to tax payers – could come under such an umbrella.

The attorney general has asked in the Supreme Court whether privacy is a fundamental right. The government's chief lawyer has also stated that 'The concept of absolute right over one's body was a myth and there were various laws which put restrictions on such a right'.[30] The contention is borne out by previous judgements, as also by some laws that impinge on the concept of absolute right over the body. But the question remains: of the safety of roughly 3MB of human biometrics and about the privacy rights of the person who is identified by it.

Epilogue

Preceding and following the fears of data protection, and in the absence of a privacy law, is an unstated question: can the Aadhaar platform be converted into a snoop stall? And a possible counter question: does the government need Aadhaar in order to snoop on its citizens?

The Indian state already has multiple institutions and instruments to intercept and act on what it perceives as acts inimical to the sovereignty of the nation. In terms of institutions and capacity, there is the IB, CBI, Military Intelligence, the NatGrid, the National Technical Research Organisation, the arms of revenue intelligence, besides local police intelligence. In terms of legal provisions, there is the Indian Telegraph Act, 1885; the Indian Telegraph Rules, 1951; the Information Technology Act 2000, within which are the Information Technology (Procedure and Safeguards for Interception; Monitoring and Decryption of Information) Rules 2009; Information Technology (Procedure and Safeguards for Monitoring and Collecting Data or Information) Rules 2009; Information Technology (Reasonable Security Practices and Procedures and Sensitive Personal Data and Information) Rules 2011; and Information Technology Guidelines for Cyber Café Rules 2011. There is also the Code of Criminal Procedure Code, 1973.

There are numerous clauses in the laws, and windows in various rules, which can be enabled for surveillance: Section 3 (1AA) Indian Telegraph Act, 1885; Rule 419 A of the Indian Telegraph Rules 1951; Section 68, 28, 29 of the Information Technology Act; Rule 6 of IT Rules, 2011. There is also sufficient institutional capacity for the government to tap into data, get metadata from internet service providers and listen in on telephone calls – a May 2014 RTI response revealed that nearly 9,000 telephone taps were authorised every month by the Central government.[31] It also has internet monitoring capacity. In November 2009, the government informed Parliament it was setting up 'a centralised system to monitor communications on mobile phones, landlines and the internet in the country'.[32] There are, in addition, offshore capabilities and capacity, and agreements with various governments on sharing data for intelligence.

The Aadhaar Act 2016 allows the government to seek disclosure of information 'including identity information or authentication records, made in the interest of national security in pursuance of a direction of an officer not below the rank of Joint Secretary to the Government of India specially authorised in this behalf by an order of the Central Government' with the proviso that every direction for information would be reviewed by a committee consisting of the cabinet secretary and secretaries of Department of Legal Affairs and Department of Electronics and Information Technology, before it takes effect.[33] Does this provision enable the UIDAI platform to be deployed for surveillance? It is a matter of interpretation. Disclosure, yes, but not surveillance as it is generally known and feared.

Fact is, the UIDAI system is a passive identification

Epilogue

platform and can only be used for authentication; the architecture and design preclude conversion. Its database only has minimal demographic data and individual biometrics. The Aadhaar Act limits the nature of data collected, as also the purpose and scope of queries. While the Aadhaar number is known to the bank, to the Income Tax Department, the telecom company et al, the Aadhaar platform itself does not have information about bank accounts or income tax returns. All authentications are yes/no answers and eKYC allows viewing of demographic data on queries but requires approval for use, and every query is a single-use query.

In a sense, the UIDAI platform is a one-way valve. Surveillance requires connecting of the small dots to get the big picture. This means that all the places where the Aadhaar number is seeded would have to be brought under one data-mining exercise for extraction of hidden predictive information from large databases. Yes, the government can access authentication records, but for anything more, it would have to go back to the many pods where the data rests and any change would require legislative sanction.

Realistically, therefore, using Aadhaar would be an arduous way to snoop when more convenient options exist. Governments across the world are already tapping into data and metadata. The scent of what was imagined by Franz Kafka in *The Trial*, by George Orwell in *1984* is here, this is Aldous Huxley's *Brave New World* in many ways. What was fantasy a few years back is reality today.

Epilogue

The technology that seemed like fiction in *Enemy of the State*, *Minority Report*, *The Conversation* and *Gattaca* is here. Agencies may be able to, like in *The Bourne Supremacy*, pick up one word off the air via satellite. Remote control of mobile phones for audio, like in *The Dark Knight*, or of cameras, is not implausible.

The internet has, in the past decade, moved on from being a medium for decentralised connectivity, even anonymous interactions. It is now a universe where data packets capture behaviour, location, transactions, which technology can track to link – and leverage – behaviour and connections across billions of users. The users are corporates, governments, academic institutions, researchers. While there is anonymisation of data in theory, processing power allows for the creation of personal profiles from seemingly impersonal information. What is personal is no longer definable.

In the digital world, Big Data is the Big Brother. The digital world is a running documentary in production starring you and your life – who you are, where you are, what you like, what you buy, who you meet. Mobile phones keep a record, via pings to the towers, on where you are and where you have been and how fast you were travelling. Google knows where you have been, what you search for; it can build a profile of your age, gender and, most recently, where you have been shopping, not just online but offline too. Facebook knows your friends, what you read, your likes, and how happy you are, based on your activity. YouTube knows what you have been watching, Netflix knows what you like to watch, Ola and Uber have your travel records, e-commerce sites know what you bought and what you are looking for.

Each and every day, individuals using or carrying any chip-enabled and connected device are emitting data exhaust for analysers. The surge in computing power – for instance, from graphics processing units which were originally developed for video games – is driving data analytics. Using a combination of cloud computing and artificial intelligence, companies are able to sift through data, analyse real time unstructured information and generate profiles and predictions by making intelligent inferences about preferences and behaviours. What you click or view is a valuable business asset across platforms. Behavioural data analytics is being used to profile users by cursor movement, browsing data is mined to know who is pregnant so that they may be targeted with focussed advertising, and even draw a risk matrix for insurers, credit card companies, banks and law enforcement agencies. Knowingly and unknowingly, you are leaving data with mobile operators, internet service providers and other companies. Estimates of the quantity of mine-worthy data are in zettabytes – the equivalent of 250 billion DVDs.[34]

These concerns were eloquently expressed in an open letter published on 28 March 2017, on the twenty-eighth birthday of the World Wide Web, by its inventor Tim Berners-Lee. 'As our data is then held in proprietary silos, out of sight to us, we lose out on the benefits we could realise if we had direct control over this data, and chose when and with whom to share it. What's more, we often do not have any way of feeding back to companies what data we'd rather not share – especially with third parties – the T&Cs are all or nothing.' The risks are multiplied in countries with authoritarian regimes, where collaboration between companies and governments can put citizens' lives at risk.[35]

Your digital trail is rich and deep, almost tailor-made for surveillance

●

To ensure and enshrine privacy as a right, especially in an event-driven contextually dynamic world, it is important to define what constitutes privacy. The idea of privacy is largely a private construct, a right in most cultures and a notion in some. At its most fundamental, privacy is about life, liberty, the right to be an autonomous person; it is about personhood. The roots of the concept can be traced to sociological and anthropological debates, and to Aristotle's reference to private domain. In Western democracies, the institutional roots of the concept are hosted in the charter of liberties known as the Magna Carta, in the Bill of Rights drafted into the US Constitution by James Madison and others and articulated by Thomas Jefferson as 'unalienable rights to life, liberty and the pursuit of happiness'.

The idea itself is continually in transition. Samuel Warren and Louis Brandeis, scholars and legal

Epilogue

luminaries, in 1890, described it as the protection of personal space and the right 'to be let alone', a phrase borrowed from Judge Thomas Cooley's famous treatise on torts in 1880. In more modern times, in 1967, Alan Westin, author of *Privacy and Freedom*, held that few values were as fundamental for society as privacy: 'Privacy is the claim of individuals, groups, institutions to determine for themselves when, how, and to what extent information about them is communicated to others.'[36] In 1992, Ferdinand Schoeman, author of *Philosophical Dimensions of Privacy: An Anthology* elaborated that privacy has broad and narrow conceptions and that at the narrow end 'privacy relates exclusively to personal information and describes the extent to which others have access to this information'.[37]

There is little doubt that principles are influenced by circumstance and context. In the United States, the Social Security Number (SSN) was created in 1936 for the purpose of tracking the earnings of workers and their linkage with benefits. Over a period, the SSN expanded to encompass numerous purposes including financial institutions, universities, health care entities and government agencies like the Internal Revenue Service. For decades, people, lawmakers and activists agitated for a law to guard privacy but couldn't secure it despite the fact that the Fourth, Fifth and Ninth Amendments ordain it.

Then came Watergate with President Nixon's ordering, and overseeing, of spying on citizens. Introducing the bill

Epilogue

On 1 May 1974, Senator Samuel James 'Sam' Ervin Jr, who had been a part of committees that investigated the Joseph McCarthy and Watergate scandals, said, 'If we have learned anything in this last year of Watergate, it is that there must be limits upon what the Government can know about each of its citizens. Each time we give up a bit of information about ourselves, we give up some of our freedom.'[38] The Privacy Act of 1974 was finally enacted on 31 December 1974.

The context changed post the 9/11 terror attacks on America. On 23 October 2001, as Rep James F. Sensenbrenner introduced the Uniting and Strengthening America by Providing Appropriate Tools Required to Intercept and Obstruct Terrorism Act aka USA Patriot Act 2001, his introductory remarks reflected the shift in context. 'We are uncertain who the enemy is. We are uncertain where the enemy is. We are more uncertain than ever before when and what the next move of the enemy will be.' This bipartisan legislation, he added, 'will give law enforcement new weapons to fight this new kind of war'.[39] Listed across 132 pages were wide-ranging powers to law enforcement agencies to tackle the threat of terrorism.

By mid-2006, the mood had changed again. The US government faced growing global and local criticism of its methods. Liberals and conservatives questioned why the war against terrorism, which was meant to preserve freedom, was instead leading to abrogation of civil liberties. The US government even as it extended

Epilogue

the Patriot Act in 2011 (of time-bound sunset clauses) set in motion the process to bring a new law. In October 2013, the Obama administration introduced the Uniting and Strengthening America by Fulfilling Rights and Ending Eavesdropping, Dragnet-collection and Online Monitoring Act aka USA Freedom Act, which was enacted in June 2015. The expanded form of the acronyms PATRIOT and FREEDOM best reflect the change in context.

The need to be secure, shielded and the desire to be left alone are inversely, and yet interminably, linked. Much depends on the elasticity of public expectations, on how much liberty people want to keep or cede – the context is not a determinant but an influencer of this elasticity. Indisputably, society at large has come to see and defend privacy as a cluster of entitlements that gives individuals the right to control information about the self, to protect their personal decisions and lifestyles from public gaze. The issue most often is about the appropriateness of appropriation.

This question is essentially a contest between views best expressed by English philosophers Hobbes and Locke. In his 1651 tome *Leviathan*, Thomas Hobbes writes about the war of 'every man against every man'[40] and proposes ceding the 'Right of Governing myself' in return for sovereign protection, an absolutist government to keep people from abusing property and privacy.[41] John Locke, a deeply private person, who would use invisible ink and a kind of shorthand to write his ideas,[42] presents the idea of personhood, self-ownership, societal respect for privacy, where the state exists to secure life, property and liberty of people. Critical to this position is the concept of consent.

In India, the founding fathers of the Constitution did not explicitly provide for the right of privacy. However, it is implicitly provided for as a part of the right to life and personal liberty as well as freedom of expression and movement, and there is also a common law right to privacy emanating from the right to property. Indeed, there is reflection of this concern in the debates in the Constituent Assembly, especially in the discussions on 'Rights of Freedom'. Somnath Lahiri, a member of the Constituent Assembly, sought that 'The privacy of correspondence shall be inviolable and may be infringed only in cases provided by law.'[43] In the modern age, the phrase 'correspondence' would arguably cover concerns about privacy of conversation, communication and perhaps all that is data.

It is pertinent to note that, as a nation, India has not shied away from endorsing privacy as a human right. India is a signatory to the UN 1948 Universal Declaration of Human Rights which states, 'No one shall be subjected to arbitrary interference with his privacy, family, home or correspondence, nor to attacks upon his honour and reputation. Everyone has the right to the protection of the law against such interference or attacks.'[44] India is also a signatory of the International Convention on Civil and Political Rights of December 1966.

Epilogue

The right for privacy has been the subject of many cases in courts across the country. The interpretation of law on the right to privacy has varied from judge to judge and judgement to judgement. The point worth noting is that while there is no explicit provision in law, the essence of the right has been accepted in some judgements. The arguments have been largely based on Article 19 (1) (d) which guarantees 'free movement through India', Article 21 which says 'no person shall be deprived of life or personal liberty except according to procedure established by law'. The question is also before the Supreme Court in separate cases filed by petitioners against the government's attempts to make Aadhaar mandatory.

The position that a law for privacy does not exist may, arguably, be legally defensible. The constant refrain is that the Constitution does not explicitly state the right. But neither does it explicitly deny it. Rights are drawn from on globally accepted principles, in philosophy and in law. The Ninth Amendment in the oldest democracy, the United States, states that 'the enumeration in the Constitution of certain rights shall not be construed to deny or disparage others retained by the people'.[45] The larger question, therefore, is: Can a modern democracy afford to not have the right to privacy?

The urgency dictating the call for a law is driven by private aspirations and public concern. India, at \$2 trillion-plus, is among the world's large economies and there is no escaping the path of digitisation ahead.

Epilogue

India has 1,150,000 Aadhaar card holders, over a billion mobile phone users, 450 million internet users. The emphasis to promote cashless transactions through apps, paperless validation through Digi Lockers and presenceless governance via online systems will find millions more online. Already data spewed out includes billions of e-authentications by UIDAI, transactions across private and public platforms – between April and June 2017, there were 274 million transactions on DBT alone and cumulatively over Rs 2 trillion was transferred in 282 schemes by forty-nine ministries.[46] As India and Indians expand their engagement and more people log on, they will communicate, transact, store and experience the digital world much more intensely, they will emit personal identifiable information. Aggravating anxieties is the reality that data moves seamlessly across public and private domains. In the absence of a law for data protection and privacy, the potential for social, political and economic disruption is immense and very real.

It is fortuitous that the angst about Aadhaar has erupted. This gives Indians an opportunity to reflect on safeguards, on who knows what about their finances, health, leisure and political activities, whether it is the digital colonisers of the corporate world with a yen for monopoly control or the state which has the monopoly over coercive powers.

Who owns what data and is sharing it with whom was brought up as a concern before the Supreme Court in April this year. The attorney general indicated that the government would bring in a law.[47] The government's willingness to enact a law for data protection was confirmed later.[48] Fact is, data protection cannot be achieved without a law on privacy; implicit in the acceptance of the need for one is the necessity for the other. The point is not the interpretation of law but the understanding of the need.

What would be the ideal template for a law on data protection and privacy?

There is no ready role model. But there are some good templates to consider. The US model, which has an omnibus privacy law and a patchwork quilt for data protection with sector-specific and state-specific regulations, the EU General Data Protection Regulation Act, the Federal Data Protection Act of Germany, the French Loi Informatique et Libertés (incorporating EU norms) and the umbrella of privacy law provisions in California. There is also an Indian avatar which B.J. Panda, BJD MP from Kendrapara in Odisha, proposes to move as a private member's bill. Context, and acceptance of its fluidity, is critical, so *ab initio* the design ought to accommodate provisions for periodic reviews and updates – to take into account rapidly changing technology and emerging practices.

Establishing the primary precept is critical for the creation of a data and privacy law. John Stuart Mill sets the bar high when he says, 'the only purpose for which power can be rightfully exercised over any member of

Epilogue

a civilised community, against his will, is to prevent harm to others'.[49] The principle must be about securing persons, relationships and decisions – freedom of choice, free will is the heartbeat of democracy. The core, as we have established before, must be about personhood, about the individual and not just a data consumer. The basis for trust rests on transparency, limitations, minimal collection of data and optimal ignorance of the system about the person. Rights would have to be explicitly guaranteed and data protection must be by design and default.

The essence of data protection and privacy stems from the definition of what constitutes personal identifiable information as also norms for anonymisation, usage and sharing. It would also have to include limitations of collection, purpose and usage with provisions for 'pseudonymising' and securing the rights of the vulnerable – children and the elderly. The means of collection ought to be fair and lawful, the purpose and relevance clearly stated, user limitations accompanied by the need for intelligible consent requirements and subject to safeguards against risks such as loss, unauthorised access, modification and disclosure. Any oversight committee of government, which sanctions use of data for investigations, needs to be subject to disclosure norms and answerable to Parliament.

Central to all of this is the principle of accountability. Laws are by definition justiciable, but securing justice requires the process to be time-bound. As evidenced in

Epilogue

many instances, policies keep evolving and expanding even as the relevant questions and cases are still pending in courts. These delays mock the petitioner. The big question is: who does the individual go to? And who will be responsible in case of reputational damage, loss of confidentiality, harm to professional secrecy or reversal of anonymisation? Real-time disclosure of breach in data safety is a *sine qua non*. The law must enshrine the individual's right to know and enable the right to opt out and be forgotten if data is misused or misappropriated – this would include profiling of dominion, beliefs, ideology. As mentioned earlier, the right to opt out of Aadhaar, without prejudice to rights and entitlements, is before the Supreme Court, and a provision to be let alone following misuse/abuse merits consideration. The principle of accountability encompasses right to avenues for the individual to petition for directions, for cease and desist orders, in cases of invasion of privacy. Whether it is UIDAI or a private entity, it is critical that the individual retains the right to seek compensation and justice. This would require a carefully considered structure and clearly spelt out regulations.

Enforcement of promises calls for the creation of an autonomous authority – say the Commission for Data Protection and Privacy. Regulations must empower the Commission to obtain information, to enforce compliance, to prohibit transfer of data and order investigations. The Commission must also be provided

Epilogue

with the resources to appoint independent auditors to probe violations and powers to legally enforce the rights of individuals to rectify, remove and block incorrect data. The Commission must be accountable to Parliament via a Standing Committee of Parliament. The fear of state overreach most certainly needs to be addressed – with norms and transparency.

Personhood is the essence of the construct of democracy. It deserves enshrinement, in spirit and letter, the fixing of fault lines, as also a comprehensive law for data and privacy protection. Without these covenants, India could be denied its true 12-digit revolution.

Notes

Scan this QR code to access the detailed notes

Acknowledgements

I am grateful to all who helped me to understand, informed me with their insights.

Thank you, President Pranab Mukherjee, Prime Minister Narendra Modi, former Prime Minister Manmohan Singh, former Finance Ministers P. Chidambaram and Yashwant Sinha, and Congress Vice President Rahul Gandhi.

I must thank Nandan Nilekani for sharing his experiences and all at UIDAI – Ram Sewak Sharma, K. Ganga, Shankar Maruwada, Sanjay Jain, Viral Shah, Naman Pugalia and others for their help and inputs. I am obliged to Omita Paul, Venu Rajamony, K.P. Krishnan, Rajesh Jain, Somasekhar S. and Milind Deora for sparing time and connecting me with people. Special thanks to Rajiv Lal and Reuben Abraham at IDFC Institute for hosting my research. And to V.K. Karthika for being so on-the-ball for this book. Thank you to Govindraj Ethiraj and Shyamlal Yadav for sharing notes, reports and tapes.

I get by with the help of my friends. Shah, Sharma and Shelgikar – Jayesh, Shravan and Sanjeev. Bimal Parekh, my host, and Sharada Harihar, my dost. Pinki Virani, my wife, this book could not have been written without you by my side.

About the Author

Shankkar Aiyar is a prominent India-based political economy analyst, columnist and author. His pathbreaking book *Accidental India* fetched him acclaim as a public intellectual. A journalist for over three decades, Aiyar has covered every parliamentary election since 1984. His 1991 scoop on India pledging its gold reserves drew world attention to the crisis in the economy which consequently compelled liberalisation. Aiyar has analysed every budget since liberalization. As a columnist, Aiyar specialises in the interface of politics and economics. He has authored a study on India's socio-economic fault lines and its hundred worst districts. His investigation on twenty-five years of political corruption is part of an anthology. He has been a Wolfson Chevening Fellow at Cambridge University where he studied the lifecycles of emerging economies. Aiyar is a Visiting Fellow at the IDFC Institute.

HarperCollins *Publishers* India

At HarperCollins India, we believe in telling the best stories and finding the widest readership for our books in every format possible. We started publishing in 1992; a great deal has changed since then, but what has remained constant is the passion with which our authors write their books, the love with which readers receive them, and the sheer joy and excitement that we as publishers feel in being a part of the publishing process.

Over the years, we've had the pleasure of publishing some of the finest writing from the subcontinent and around the world, including several award-winning titles and some of the biggest bestsellers in India's publishing history. But nothing has meant more to us than the fact that millions of people have read the books we published, and that somewhere, a book of ours might have made a difference.

As we look to the future, we go back to that one word— a word which has been a driving force for us all these years.

Read.

Harper Collins Publishers India

At HarperCollins India, we forever marvel at the happiness gained finding the 'understandership' for any book, or every human readable. We started publishing in 1992, a sign that has changed since then, but what has remained constant is the passion with which our authors write their books, the love with which readers receive them, and the care and excitement that we as publishers feel in being a part of the publishing process.

Sure, we too, won't lead the pleasure of publishing some of the finest writing talents in the continent and around the world, including several award-winning titles and some of the biggest bestsellers in India publishing history. But nothing has come close to us than the fact that many people have read the books we published, and that somewhere, a book of ours might have made a difference.

As we look to the future, we go back to that one word—a word which has been a part of us for over half these years.

Read.